LECTURES

ON THE

PANTHEISTIC IDEA

OF

AN IMPERSONAL-SUBSTANCE-DEITY,

AS CONTRASTED WITH

THE CHRISTIAN FAITH CONCERNING
ALMIGHTY GOD.

BY THE
REV. MORGAN DIX, S. T. D.
RECTOR OF TRINITY CHURCH, NEW YORK.

NEW YORK:
PUBLISHED BY HURD AND HOUGHTON,
BOSTON: E. P. DUTTON AND COMPANY.
1864.

RIVERSIDE, CAMBRIDGE:
STEREOTYPED AND PRINTED BY
H. O. HOUGHTON AND COMPANY.

ADVERTISEMENT.

THE following Lectures were prepared in the early part of last year, and were delivered at St. Paul's Chapel during the Lenten season of 1863. They were preached, for the second time, in Trinity Chapel, during the past winter, at the request of a large number of the members of our parish. After that, the Vestry of Trinity Church expressed, by a resolution to that effect, the wish that they should be published. This desire could not be acceded to without embarrassment; for the lectures were written without reference to publication, and the author, while aware of the character and extent of their imperfections, knew also that he had no time to make them what he would have them, and that they must go forth as they were, or not at all. But the hope that they might do good outweighed the fear of criticism, while the author felt that the known difficulties of his position would establish his claim to favorable indulgence. It is our misfortune, in this country, that we have no body of clergy sequestered for careful and holy studies in defence of the faith;

no cloistered band whose only work it should be to read and write and pray, and thereby sustain the active laborers in the open field. Till this defect be mended, the out-door workers must be also the writers, notwithstanding all the disadvantages of their situation. But while it is so, they should be treated with allowance, and judged not so much in respect to the manner in which they accomplish their tasks, as with reference to the object and end proposed. The priests of the Church, in the full exercise of their functions, can hardly be expected to have time to write at all; much less can it be thought that they should be able to write with careful and polished style, and with the finish and refinement which come of leisure for practice and discipline. But reputation is the last object which we may propose to ourselves who have upon us, day by day, the care of the souls of sinners: only to the good of those souls may we look, and to the glory of Almighty God. Enough if the former of these ends be secured, and the latter in any degree promoted; the writer will cheerfully bear the reproach of those who may read, not to grow better and wiser, but to find occasions against the theme in the shortcomings of him who handles it. What has been written and preached, and is now given to the public, was so prepared and spoken solely with the view of stating the truth concerning the Almighty. May He accept the work done unto His honor; and may He forgive the weakness of His servant, and bring, as He ever does, spiritual strength out of mortal infirmity. Unto Him be glory everlastingly. Amen.

TRINITY RECTORY, New York, *May* 23, 1864.

CONTENTS.

INTRODUCTION.

ALTHOUGH it is considered that the design of the following Lectures could hardly be misunderstood by one who should read them without prejudice, yet it seems proper to meet one objection which may be thought by some to lie against them. The writer would, therefore, in advance disclaim the intention of fixing upon every one whose theories on history, on ethics, and on the course and movement of terrestrial things, are in the following pages more particularly referred to, the stigma and reproach of consciously holding the philosophical system with which those theories are undoubtedly allied. For it is a well-known feature of the pantheistic heresy, and characteristic of that profound spiritual disease, that the very individuals whose views most nearly harmonize with it may yet be strenuous in disclaiming the relationship, although it be evident that their position is a complete inconsequence, except as interpreted on the hypothesis of such a tie. We are willing, then, to admit and to give prominence to the fact of their protests and denials, thinking it sufficient to prove the identity of the results reached in either case. If the popular and plausible rationalism of the day is found to involve the same consequences which follow from the principles of simple Pantheism, that should be enough to secure for it the mistrust and aversion of thoughtful men; the question of the degree of consanguinity may be held as not essential.

The object proposed in these lectures is as follows: — To show, after stating scientifically the vast and disastrous heresy of the ages, that modern lines of thought, professed modern discoveries, and modern theories of human progress, of history, of ethics, and of religion, are but new developments of the spirit which invented that fatal system; that they run in parallel lines with it; that they lead to the same conclusions. The author entertains no doubt of the fact of this correspondence. It is not necessary to prove identity of origin: it is enough to show that the principle which underlies the whole system of modern speculation involves the results which were reached by the ancient philosophies, and that the movement is toward the very same position of a final and universal skepticism. After that, it matters little whether the writers of our day consent or decline to be classed as followers of the old pagan masters. They labor toward the same ends, and are walking in the same direction.

The grand idea of the age in which we live is

progress. That word is rung in our ears incessantly, from pulpit and platform, with the pertinacious tintinnabulation of a jangling chime. It is a progress without God, and apart from the institutions of Christianity; a progress aside from revelation and in independence of spiritual authority; the progress of humanity, confident in itself and in its own powers. The Church also announces a progress to mankind; but not a progress such as that of which the world is dreaming, and in the fancied accomplishment of which society seems fairly drunk. A progress is implied in the very idea of redemption; the prophets, the evangelists, the apostles, have spoken and written thereof, in language of unmatched sublimity; and God Himself, incarnate, has illustrated its nature and initiated it in His own person. Let us not forget that progress is the symbol of Christianity; but let us also remember of what sort that progress is: that Christ, becoming man, did grow in wisdom and in stature, and in the showing forth of love and sacrifice, until, having been made perfect therein, He was lifted up, and glorified, and set on the right hand of the Majesty on high; and that, in Christ, man is also to be in like manner elevated and exalted, yet only through grace and by the favor of God,—not for his own merits, nor in his own strength; and that he is also to grow to the measure of the stature of the fulness of Christ, and to find at length his home in heaven, and his sphere of action in eternity. This idea of progress, — through grace by faith, and in the path of sacrifice and love, — is the grand idea of Christianity. But it is not that progress which is spoken of in the world and in the philosophic and rationalistic schools. Their's is a godless progress, a merely human progress, an illusion and a dream; the speech is as sounding brass and a tinkling cymbal, and the end is disappointment and disgrace. It is so, because men do not include in their idea of progress the truth concerning the personal and living God, revealed to us in the gospel and through the Church of Jesus Christ. When that faith is lost to man, his progress is that of one who rushes headlong in the dark, and sees not the gulf toward which he is hastening.

The rationalistic schemes in vogue in our own day would seem to rest, as upon a basis, on three principles, two of which are positive and the third negative. The two positive principles are, the unity and identity of substance, and the mutable and variable character of truth. The negative principle is, the denial of the existence of any revelation aside from that which is supposed to be made to each individual through his own mind and spirit. The presence of these principles may clearly be detected, not merely in the writings of the philosophizers of the day, but also in the tendencies of our popular religionists, who have practically annulled the authority of the Word of God, by admitting in its extremest rigor the fatal right of private judgment as to the meaning of the Scriptures, and who have no more idea of a divinely established church than a barbarian has of a constitutional government. It is against that threefold basis of rationalism that we are now called to put forth all the strength we possess; and there is no work of more sacred obligation for us, at this hour, than to declare the opposite principles of the infinite and radical distinction between God and the universe; of the immutable and unvarying nature of truth, as contradistinguished from human opinions; and of the binding force and sole sufficiency of the revelation once for all made to the world by Jesus Christ, and perpetuated in the visible Church. Other themes possess but slight importance as compared with these; about them lie the issues of life death.

With one remark, in addition, these introductory observations shall be terminated. Much has been said in the following Lectures concerning the origin of the world, the course of human events, and the progress of our race. The views entertained upon the latter two of these subjects will vary according to the idea held respecting the foremost of the three. Let it then be observed that there is a crucial test of all theories of the origin of the universe. It is the Catholic dogma of the creation: "*In principio Deus creavit cœlum et terram.*" It is impossible to misconstrue those words; it is equally impossible to evade them. A man must accept them or refuse them. If he hold them frankly and honestly, he cannot be a pantheist. If, on the other hand, he stagger at them, and hesitate about receiving them, he is not to be depended upon. And if any one deny them outright, we maintain that there is for him no possible choice save between the schemes of Dualism and Pantheism. The dogma of the creation, as opposed to the hypothesis of emanation or that of development, — a dogma sublime above all others, as well as first of all in order, — is declared to us in the Scriptures and secured to us in the Creed, to the end that we may be forever settled and established in the truth; that the dark problem, against which the unenlightened mind has ever dashed itself in fruitless striving, may be cleared up; that we may have a rational and satisfying cosmogony; and that the whole of life may be rendered real and practical and comprehensible to man. When that dogma is denied, all is in effect denied. When the belief in a God who created the world has been lost, all is lost that is stable or permanent in human thought. If the theories to which reference is hereinafter made can be reconciled with the first article of the

Christian faith, we are ready to withdraw our objections to those schemes. But if, on the contrary, it be found impossible to harmonize them with that article, we charge them with being radically antichristian; and we shall classify them with the great traditional heresy of the ages, until cause be shown why they should not be assigned to that stock, and until it be proved that, as to leading ideas and practical results, they are not substantially one and the same with it.

LECTURES.

LECTURE I.

THE CHURCH AND PHILOSOPHY.

THE seasons of Advent and Lent have been from very ancient time regarded in the Church of Christ as especially suitable for the work of instructing the people in the higher mysteries of the Faith. There are at those times strong, though silent, influences about us which affect the heart with unusual force, and dispose to a more thoughtful attention to the word of life; and the power of the Spirit is upon us then in fuller measure and with more evident effect. Accordingly it is purposed, by God's permission, to devote a part of this season of Lent to studies of the class referred to, by means of a course of lectures, in which the subject shall be the EXISTENCE OF ALMIGHTY GOD.

They who watch and comprehend the current of modern thought, will not feel surprised at my choice of a theme. For the great question of our day is about the Personality of the Deity, with all that the term implies. It is not in dispute whether there be, or be not, a God; but whether the God, whose existence is in terms admitted, be, or be not, a Personal God. Upon this point the controversy is joined. On the one hand, we find a series of propositions, clear and intelligible, concerning the Almighty Being, in which are included affirmations touching His eternity, His providence, His acts in the past, His purposes in the future, and His relations to the universe and to mankind. This body of doctrine is formulated in the Creed of the Catholic Church. On the other hand, there may be noticed a class of expressions, variable, misty, vague, and unintelligible, concerning a somewhat which is, for convenience' sake, styled God. These constitute a kind of tissue in which are packed the religious thoughts of the free-thinkers and rationalizers of the period. It is proposed in the following lectures to contrast these two ideas of the Deity, so far as the looseness of the latter will permit: — to compare the dogma and the speculation, the substance and the shadow, the truth and the fable, the reality and the dream.

In position, in importance, and in necessity, this subject stands second to none.

In position; because the question about the existence of Almighty God precedes all others that can be raised whether in religion or in philosophy.

In importance; because He hath none that may be compared with Him, and we, without Him, are less than nothing.

In necessity; because of the rashness, the levity, the ignorance with which His being, His attributes, and His works are treated of or referred to by the writers and talkers of our day.

The task in hand is, therefore, approached with serious convictions of duty, as respects the honor of the Almighty and the safety of the souls of men. If He be what He is represented to be in the Creed, then is the rationalistic conception of Him an outrage on His majesty and a libel on His name. If, on the other hand, the Rationalists are correct, then are we Christians the victims of a delusion, and our hope in Him, our love for Him, our fear of Him, are but phases of childish superstition.

Let me open this great theme, by drawing a clear and sharp distinction. It is the distinction between the Church and Philosophy. All who think and believe as the Church instructs us, have a faith; while they who think and speculate independently of her definitions, can rise no higher than the level of a probable opinion. A faith is the gift of God to us in the Church; while the suggestion of an opinion is the highest attainment of Philosophy.

The Church has her Creed. It is unvariable and fixed. It has come to us from the earliest days. That Creed, so far as it relates to the Most High and undivided Trinity, is held (and we rejoice to remember this) by multitudes who are not externally in union with us. When, therefore, I speak of the faith, I mean the belief in God which is expressed in that Creed; and all who think of Him as He is therein described, we place together as holding, so far forth, the Church view, the Christian idea.

Upon the other side we set all those persons who hold opinions at variance with the articles of the Creed, and we comprehend their views under the general name of philosophy. We do this, remembering that the themes of philosophy, in the highest sense of the word, are the same as those of theology; that the chief studies of the ancient philosophers were about God, man, the soul, our duties, and our destinies; and that it is possible to speculate on these subjects independently of revelation. Opinions about Almighty God, when formed and held without reference to the Creed of the Church, may be termed, without harshness, philosophical opinions; and their maintainers we regard, not as believers, but as philosophers. There were schools of philosophy in the time of our Lord and his apostles; St. Paul refers to them and warns the faithful against them. There are schools of philosophy now, in our own day, and in our own land, and in our very midst; and we, who stand upon the apostolic platform, must bear our witness against them. The modern schools have as little authority as the ancient; whatever they may call themselves, we owe them no more deference or respect.

We class, therefore, under the head of philosophic speculation all those views which differ from the standards of the Church ; and we say, that if a man believes the Creed, he has a faith, and that if he denies it he has a philosophy. And so, in the philosophic schools of the period, we shall find ideas very different from those entertained and taught in the Church. We shall find the particular views of men, stated with grace of diction, presented with plausibility, defended by weighty arguments, asserted with zeal, full often recommended by the pure and moral lives of their maintainers. But yet we shall feel that these men are offering us a philosophy and not a faith ; and that if we were to exchange what we have received for what they would give we should be bartering confidence for hesitation, assurance for doubt, and humble trust in Another for reliance in self.

To these philosophic schools must we go, however, in order to learn what are the opinions of men concerning Almighty God. Nor shall we reck, though among these schools there be some whose members style them Christian churches, and propose their own speculative theories for consideration as Christian doctrine. On the contrary, we shall regard such claims as but additional instances of groundless opinions on the part of their maintainers. To hear such claims need cause us no surprise, for it seems the most natural thing in the world that they should be made. If men entertain erroneous views of God, of Christ, of sin, of redemption, it would seem to follow of necessity that their views respecting themselves should also be incorrect. Since the philosophic schools, exhibiting no stability, vary incessantly in their opinions about Almighty God, we cannot count as better than an opinion the special views which they may hold concerning their own corporate character. We shall, therefore, go to them, whatever they may style themselves, as we would go to schools of opinion, which in fact they are; and from them we shall learn how the human mind thinks of God, when that mind has shaken itself free from the restraints of law and has rejected the traditions of the past. We shall then compare these results with the articles of faith as taught, the same everywhere and always, in the Church; and thus we shall obtain the double advantage, first, of a clearer view of the truth, and secondly, of a more loving appreciation of its worth and power.

But a difficulty may suggest itself to the mind of some one here present; a question may arise upon the design which has been announced. To some it may appear as though the subject chosen for these lectures were too simple a one to admit of protracted discussion. It might be said, all men, or almost all, believe in God. All admit His existence; all do Him reverence, and confess their obligation to obey Him. Why then select a theme about which there is practically so little variance among men? Why not rather choose some subject distinctly characteristic of the system of the Church?

Alas, my hearers, these are but assumptions. To name the name of God is not enough; to say that a man believes in Him is not enough; to admit His existence is not sufficient. The name which you give Him must be His own name, and not the name of another. The faith in Him must not be an erroneous faith, but a true one. The confession of His existence must accord with the sublime facts of His eternal nature and being. There be gods many and lords many in these days, but unto us there is only the one God, the very and the true. The doctrine of Almighty God is indeed the first of all; but there, at the threshold and at its mere announcement, men stumble and fall. Count not too surely on the correctness of any one's conceptions of Him until you know how those conceptions have been formed; whether the mind has humbled itself before His word, or whether the will has marked out for itself a path, and struck away therein. There is not perhaps a greater want at this hour, a deeper want, a more urgent want, among our people, than that of a true and right knowledge of God. Even from the first has man erred therein. Our first parents doubted of Him; they mistook His character, and in that error they disbelieved His word. And this they did, although He was with them as a father and a friend, although He communed with them face to face, and called them by their names. It is a strange and a most instructive picture. With them, day by day; accustomed to walk with them among the trees of the garden; wont to reason with them and to teach them, as a parent deals with the child: not even then did the Lord God succeed in impressing on their minds and hearts a correct idea of Himself. They mistook Him altogether. They thought, "He will not keep His word; and, though He promise, yet He will not perform." And so, they considered, that they might with impunity taste the forbidden fruit, although He had declared in their ears, "in the day that thou eatest thereof, thou shalt surely die." If then, in Eden, and ere yet they had fallen from original righteousness, our first parents had and acted on a false impression of God, notwithstanding the advantage of a habitual, a most intimate intercourse and communion with Him; — let us not marvel that aberrations should be found to-day, and every day, and everywhere on this subject; aberrations in the course of human thought, as men plod wearily through the world. Error there is, on this first point, on this fundamental truth; error, wide-spread and profound. It shall be shown to you; it shall be set before you, in its deepest shades of gloom; and you shall see what horrible heresies have arisen to hide from our eyes the Lord God Almighty, Creator of heaven and earth. You shall hear of schemes of doctrine in which the true idea of Him has vanished, although His name be, for decency's sake, retained. And then the ramifications of error shall be traced; its influence pointed out; its tracks and footprints noted in places where they were unsuspected; until you feel that for want of knowledge of this first article of the Creed, multitudes are in actual and extreme peril; and until you thank the good Lord for preserving us from the calamity of losing the truth, as many in our midst have lost it forever.

To proceed. The observations already made have been but preliminary. It was intended to introduce by them the subject to which your close attention is to be called. And in order to show in what course we are to journey together, I would next remark, that there exists, and has existed from very ancient days, a certain infidel theory which, though not widely taught at the present time in its scientific form, underlies most of the popular errors of the day. It concerns the nature and manner of existence of Almighty God, and it may be regarded as the just expression of the cast of modern philosophic thought on those mysteries. I refer to the system commonly known as Pantheism. That system will form the subject of our studies; and you are now invited to a comparative view of the philosophic theory known as Pantheism, and of the Christian faith as contained in the Creeds of the Catholic Church. The discussion will be arranged as follows: —

In the next lecture, it is proposed to state the system of Pantheism in its crude, its abstract, its theoretic form.

In the third lecture of the course, I shall endeavor to show under what shapes, and in what quarters we meet with that system in its practical operation; for in its theoretic form, it is, as yet, hardly known or admitted amongst us.

In the fourth lecture, the consequences and results of the theory will be pointed out; since in these we find our strongest arguments against it.

The fifth lecture will be devoted to the presentation of the Christian ideas of Almighty God, as gathered from that revelation of Himself which He has made to us through His eternal Son.

And, in the sixth, and closing lecture, we shall contrast the life of one who holds the pantheistic scheme with that of the believer, and exhibit the probable working of the two systems in the way of this mortal existence and at the hour of death.

And now may the Holy Spirit, whose aid and blessing we invoke, guide the preacher and the hearer into the fuller knowledge and deeper love of the truth.

In bringing these introductory observations to a conclusion, two suggestions will be made on points connected with our general subject.

The first is this: that while the word Pantheism is very frequently used, the system known by that name is but imperfectly understood. And hence it has come to pass that careless, ignorant, or interested speakers allow themselves the widest latitude in its employment; while the ordinary hearer gathers from it only a vague and uncertain impression of evil because he knows not precisely what it means. It is convenient for the unlearned to have within reach some high-sounding term, with which to lay about him, in emergencies, to the surprise and alarm of the vulgar. In this manner, the term "Pantheism" has been employed. When the partisan does not know precisely what to say against some dogma or some view which he regards as erroneous or unsound, he cries out, as a last resort, that it is pantheistic, trusting with that wordy blast to make an end. But such a charge, although it may at first alarm, through its power of suggesting a freight of unknown horrors, soon ceases to terrify, especially if too frequently repeated; for the people, attaching no very precise idea to the word, are not likely to feel the proper degree of abhorrence for things pantheistic, because they do not know what Pantheism is. Full often has the preacher heard this term employed in a loose, impracticable way, and in cases where there was no ground at all for the charge. For this reason, the attempt will be made to give a clear definition of the word and an intelligible account of the system. If that attempt should prove successful, the result will follow, that, while you recoil from that dark, that gloomy, that hopeless theory with the deepest horror, you will at the same time have formed too clear an idea of it to be in danger of tracing it or thinking that you see it where it is not. The remark has been made of a certain great commentator on the Holy Scriptures, deceased some two centuries ago, that he was crazed on the subject of an early sect of heretics known as the Gnostics, so that there was hardly a chapter in St. Paul's Epistles, in which he did not think he saw allusion to gnostic opinions or gnostic error. Thus has it been in a measure with Pantheism. Men cry out that it is here, that it is there, whenever they meet with a difficulty which they are too ignorant or too lazy to grapple with and master, or whenever they would refute a doctrine unpalatable to their taste. Thus, when we speak of Christ as having the common humanity of all our race, some cry "Pantheism!" Or, when we refer to all the faithful as truly and really in Christ, and He in them, there are well-meaning folks who utter the same exclamation, because they think that they ought to make some protest, and yet can imagine nothing else to say. But, brethren, all error is not pantheistic. And our attempt to explain the system will involve an indirect defence of certain doctrines of the Church; since when you come to know what it really is, you will perceive how idle are some of those charges which are brought by sciolists against the mysteries of redemption.

The second and final suggestion for your thoughts, dear brethren in Christ, is this: that studies such as those now proposed may help to prepare us, under the blessing of God, and under the guidance of the Holy Ghost, for meeting the last danger which comes on the inhabitants of the earth, as the end of the world approaches. We are told, that, before the Lord's return to judgment, antichrist shall come. Who is antichrist? and what? The answer to these questions our studies in philosophy may help to furnish. Be not misled. Antichrist, it seems, is more likely to appear in the habit of a speculative philosopher than in the vestments of a pope. The real antichrist, I think, will be the reason of man; that reason in its final attitude, when, having first refused the guidance of revelation, having despised the Church and thrown away the scriptures, having theorized for itself, having sought out many inventions in the field of thought, having announced its own conclusions as the sum of all wisdom and knowledge, it stands, at length, erect and defiant, proclaiming its self-sufficiency and declaring its independence of any God above, of any law, tradition, order, faith below. Do not look for antichrist in any of the temples of the Lord; nor among men, who, however grievously they may have erred, do still in substance hold the faith. He cometh not that way. But look for him in the schools of an ungodly speculation; in the labyrinths of independent thought; in the pulpits where is preached the self-glorification of man. That is the road whereby he comes. And when, according to prophecy, the night sets in, that night of falsehood and error with which he shall obscure the knowledge of God, the Lord shall save us, if we cling to the faith once delivered to the saints, utterly refusing to have any other creed than that of ancient time. And so shall we be in peace; and we, the Israel of God, shall have light in our dwellings; while beyond there shall not be an house where there is not one dead.

LECTURE II.

PANTHEISM IN ITS THEORETIC FORM.

In the opening lecture of this course, its general subject was announced to be, a comparison between the speculative theory known as Pantheism, and the Christian faith as contained in the Creed. It is now proposed to present, in its scientific form, the theory referred to, and to show what is the pantheistic conception of God. The word has an ill-starred sound; to place it in conjunction with the symbol of the Catholic faith is to set death and life in contrast. But perhaps the term would be less appalling if better understood. Regarded at a distance, the spectre looms before us with formidable mien ; but it might yield to a vigorous blow, or even melt in the ray of a light held full in front. To those who are bewitched by Pantheism it is, indeed, as fatal an adversary as a man could encounter on his pathway. But there is actually no reason why any one should be led off by it. For it is marked by that weakness which belongs to the illogical and the absurd. It is repulsive, it is cold. It has grandeur, but that grandeur is the grandeur of obscurity. Its language is impressive, but this results from a profitless mysticism. This evening we will consider the theory in its simple and abstract form. Afterwards, its application will be pointed out, and its falseness exposed. In all this, may that blessed Spirit be our guide whose aid we still invoke!

A distinction has already been drawn between the Church and the School of Philosophy. The Church is that divinely appointed institution in and by which the simple and unalterable revelation of God is preserved in the world and everywhere presented to mankind. The Philosophic School, on the other hand, is an invention of human origin, where changeful and complex opinions are ventilated and discussed. Now, the first question in philosophy is that which touches the existence of God, and the second concerns His nature. And since the Church and the School differ mainly in this, that the latter perpetually asks questions while the former constantly instructs, the first article of the Christian faith is that which declares the existence of the Almighty, and the next is that which tells us who and what He is, and what He has done.

Philosophy, however, (and by this I mean the human reason speculating freely without reference to revelation,) admits at the outset that there is a God. To do this is doubtless unavoidable; for atheism is moral, intellectual, and spiritual death, and genuine atheists are, and always have been, and always must be, very few and very far between. Philosophy, therefore, repels with virtuous indignation the charge of denying the existence of a Deity. It has ever been so. The ancient schools and the modern were alike in this point. The epicureans and the stoics whom St. Paul encountered on Mars' Hill, acknowledged, after their own fashion, the gods. The rationalists of to-day, be they German, French, English, or American, admit the term and employ the sacred name; and among the leading heresiarchs might be mentioned some who have expended much power in framing ingenious demonstrations of a religious character to show that there is a Supreme Being, and to clear up the mystery of His nature.

It is not, therefore, on the question whether there be a God that the Church and the Philosophers join issue. So far they agree. But when they go on to speak of His nature they differ. When it is asked, "What is God?" the systems part, never to meet again.

The ground of this divergence is the total antagonism in views respecting the personality of the Deity. Does God exist as an impersonal substance, like air, or water? or has He a true personality, like men? This question is met by opposite replies.

The Church declares a personality in the Deity; a personality in the highest and fullest sense of the word. She teaches her children to believe, that as each one of them has a true, distinct, practical personality, so likewise is it with the God who made them all. Nay; she does not merely say that what is true of them is true of Him; she implies that it is true of Him in a higher sense, in a completed sense. So that, whatever may be the elements of proper personality, they exist in us but imperfectly, in Him with absolute fulness. This is the Catholic faith. Philosophy, on the other hand, opines that God has no personality; that He is an absolute, omnipresent, and impersonal substance; as it were, an atmosphere in which everything lives; a heat diffused in which everything is kept warm; an element in which everything swims. In that sense philosophy considers that there is a God, and admits that God to be eternal.

The personality of Almighty God is either in terms or by implication, incessantly denied, even by those who admit their belief in His existence. This is a phenomenon so strange as to invite to investigation. To us Christians there seems to be a contradiction here, and, although the persons to whom we refer may not be aware of the true state of the case, we cannot but conjecture that there is something behind to account for their position. The human reason, when acting in pure independence, is the least logical, the most unreasonable agent that can be named. Still, we ought not to ascribe so singular a phenomenon as that under consideration to mere caprice, unless it can be accounted for in no other way. To admit that there is a God, and yet to say that He has no personal qualities or attributes, sounds indeed, to Christian ears, like trifling ; it seems as much as to say, with one breath, that God is, and with the next, that He is not. But may there not be something behind and beyond — something to account for this apparent contradiction, to harmonize this seeming discrepancy ? May we not guess at a basis of some sort on which these statements rest, and may there not be some baleful light in which, if viewed, they will assume a horrible consistency ? I think and hope to show that this is the case; that the apparently flippant denials of God's providence, and power, and active interest and interference in our affairs, are all cognate to a philosophic scheme of great gravity and importance; that these assertions are not the assertions of levity, but the postulates of intellectual rebellion against the truth; that these opinions are not mere heterogeneous notions thrown carelessly together, or uttered just as they chance to rise to the surface in the seething-pot of this uneasy, bubbling, frothy mind of ours, but part and parcel of a well-conceived and carefully digested theory. By that theory only can they be explained. That theory is the theory of Pantheism. So that if one should ask what the popular language of the day means, and why any one should refuse to admit a personality in Almighty God, why any man should think concerning Him, not as we Christian believers think, but as if He were like unto an aeriform fluid, a gas, a force, an element, the true answer would be that the explanation of these strange notions must be sought in the theory of Pantheism. It is not, of course, intended to say that all who hold the loose speech so often heard about us accept and profess the system to which that kind of speech belongs; but we affirm that the connection between the system and the language is direct. The pantheistic theory is the proper and natural theory of intellectual philosophy regarded as independent of revelation; and by it only can these conceptions, which otherwise were mere fantastic crudities, be explained. Hence may be inferred the vast importance of an acquaintance with that execrable system; for, when once a man has mastered it he will know the real meaning of what he hears, and he shall never again be at a loss to explain these false, delusive dreams about Almighty God. For the whole system is one vast dream, one shapeless sea of gloom and woe, without light, without life, cold, remorseless, devouring — an abyss in which all honest conviction is engulfed, all manly belief buried — and the opinions to which we have referred are but the vapors of the surface of that waste, the steam from its unwholesome face.

Let us then, without delay, proceed to consider the theory of Pantheism in its abstract and philosophic form, that having measured the depth thereof, and having learned, by lead and plummet, the foulness of the slime below, we may forever abhor the system as it deserves to be abhorred, and denounce it as it ought to be denounced.

The theory of Pantheism may be thus expressed: it asserts the unity and identity of substance, and denies to the finite any real existence apart from the infinite. I hasten, however, to present these thoughts in more popular terms. It is held by the maintainers of the system now under consideration that there is only one substance throughout the universe. Of that substance everything is formed. The sea and the dry land, the mountain and the river, the bird and the beast, the flowers and the trees, the bodies and souls of men, the skies, the stars, the suns, the world, the universe throughout, all are of one and the selfsame substance. It matters not what differences or what varieties there be in form, figure, properties, or uses; all things at last are essentially one and the same. "*Unity and identity of substance.*" This is the pantheistic principle. Earth, air, fire, water, all at last, one. The ground on which you walk is substantially the same as you that walk on it. The book in which you read is of the same substance as your mind which comprehends it. This pulpit in which I preach is of the same substance as I. All things one and the same. But where is God? you ask. Ah, brethren, this one substance is God also. This substance is the only God.

But how did the world, in its present state, come into existence? That is the question which the philosophers profess to answer. They speak with contempt of the Catholic dogma of creation, styling it "The Manufacture Theory." They find it impossible to conceive of a Deity who is able to cause anything to be which was not before; and they propose to give us in place of the ridiculous idea of a production, by manufacture, as they term it, a rational, intelligible, and satisfactory explanation of the origin of the universe. Let us hear this explanation and consider how charmingly it smoothes the way before us, and how admirably it is fitted to satisfy the religious and candid mind.

The universe was not created; it came by development or emanation. Does any one comprehend what that means?

If it means anything intelligible, or if we may gather its meaning by study of the whole tenor of their thoughts, that meaning would seem to be as follows:—

There is but one single substance throughout the universe. That substance is eternal; there never was a time before which it was not. So existing from eternity, it had no personality nor any qualities, attributes, or powers, such as we understand to belong to persons and to constitute them such. It was without consciousness, without knowledge, without activity. It WAS; no more. The idea thus presented to us is that of a vast, illimitable flood; of a great, unfathomable deep; of a hollow silence, a heavy unconsciousness, a condition, mute, speechless, thoughtless. Imagine, if you can, this indescribable, this immense condition, or mass, or state, (or by whatever name you may choose to call it,) and you have before you the only eternal being. Let us apply to it, for the sake of convenience, the term God.

Such, then, from eternity; still, sombre, vast, infinite; without knowledge, or thought, or action, or result; such would this substance ever have remained but for an agency within itself. That agency was a kind of inner movement. The mass so indescribable, so incomprehensible, was agitated from within by an equally indescribable and incomprehensible motion. There was, from within, a tendency toward the surface. The great belly of blackness and unconscious horror, rumbled as it were, and the abyss, for it seems no better, was in labor and would bring forth. The result of this movement was seen in the uprising of certain definite forms and shapes. The substance, working from within, threw itself out into visible phenomena. Thus, there came forth a sky; and thus by aggregation stole forth the planets and the stars. And thus, to limit ourselves to this mundane sphere, the round world resulted from that inner force. The earth was then a part of that eternal substance, localized; a finite form of that infinite. And since that substance was God, therefore the earth was God. It was God made visible in the form of ground, and seas, and hills, and plains. The same is affirmed of all the animals. They were forms thrown out from that inner germination, all of the same substance, and all parts of God, or realizations of God.

We have next to hear the pantheistic explanation of the existence of mankind. It has been remarked that the eternal substance now spoken of and which the pantheists call God, had, at first, no knowledge and no consciousness. When, agitated by the inner motive force, it threw itself out into visible forms, as described, each of those forms expressed some tendency, some capability of this eternal substance. But as yet it had no consciousness, there was nought but a blind appetency, and a pushing forth on every hand, and a groping in and through the gloom. At length, however, the time arrived at which a higher development should take place. For out of these unconscious efforts there was at length evolved a higher form than any which had yet occurred. This new phenomenon, so thrust upward as from the inner heave and surge of the vast womb, in some manner not explained, suddenly advanced to the perception of its own existence. This fraction of the eternal substance suddenly perceived the fact expressed in the words, "I exist, I am." It saw that it was. It beheld in front of it the universe; it perceived itself to be therewith, face to face. It was conscious at length; the infinite substance thought and reasoned and took counsel with itself at last. This was, of course, God. It was God arriving at a higher development than any yet reached. It was God coming to the consciousness of Himself. When God was only that great illimitable waste, God had no knowledge of His own existence, no personality, no power. When God developed into stars, and suns, and an earth, there was as yet no personality, because they are not persons but things, and they were but the substance,—God realized in forms. When God developed into trees and animals, there were motion, and force, and appetite, and instinct, but no more. When, however, at the last, God took this higher form and passed to consciousness, then, for the first time, God saw Himself; God became fully aware of His own existence; God arrived at the knowledge of God in becoming man. Man is a developed form of the Eternal Being; he is that being reasoning, thinking, perceiving, knowing, speaking. That substance never reasoned, nor thought, nor perceived, nor knew, nor spake, before. And that substance is eternal and is the only God; and, therefore, God perceives not, nor knows, nor reasons, nor thinks, nor speaks, but in man. There is the sequence, the clear, necessary conclusion from the premises. Man is God come to consciousness of Himself; and God has no personality, and no consciousness but in man.

This, my hearers, is the philosophic theory which underlies the speculative infidelity of the present age and the present generation. I leave to another lecture the work of tracing in its indications a view too monstrous, too forbidding, to be openly and boldly taught, and would therefore limit the remainder of this evening's observations to reflection on the prospect to which that theory would invite us. Look about you, then, and consider how, according to that system, you must interpret, and how understand, the phenomena which meet your eyes. All that you behold is the one eternal substance in divers forms. There is nothing eternal but that substance. The forms are not eternal; that only is eternal of which they are made up. So that all which you see is part and parcel of God. There never was a creation. The story in Genesis about the six days is but a fable. There is no Creator, and therefore nothing was made. All things have come to be what they are in their own times and seasons by development, without a plan, without a purpose, without the guidance and direction of a mind. An impersonal and eternal substance is the only God. These outward shapes on which we look are the figures which that impersonal essence has taken, without consciousness and without method. All visible phenomena are God; God under certain conditions of size, of color, of property. Look at the dull, inert stones of the wilderness; it is God sleeping. Look at the brutes endowed with instinct, but without intellect; that is

God dreaming. Look at the thing which we call man; that is God thinking, reasoning, desiring, willing. The sky spread over all in its vaporous, palpitating blue; that is the eternal substance spreading itself forth as a firmament above. The seas slow heaving to the sunlight, or dark below the nocturnal shade; they are the same eternal substance, moaning through zone and hemisphere in blind pursuit of higher realizations. The mountain ranges, those spinal columns of this earthly frame, they are but God, the eternal substance, consolidated in progressive development. Nor may the survey cease at this point. As with material nature so with spiritual; they are one. The mind of man is substantially one with his body. The spirit, the soul, the affections, have no real existence apart from the corruptible frame in which they dwell. They are but higher manifestations of the same eternal substance, the highest to which, by inward movement, it has yet attained.* And as for all and each of these, material and immaterial, corporeal and spiritual alike, no one of them has promise or prospect of permanence, for nothing is eternal but that one universal substance, and no mind guides its development; therefore, there can be no foretelling its future directions. / The skies, the seas, the hills, may all pass away, and other formations take their place. A few years and there may be left no insect, no bird, no gentle beast. A few ages and there

* See Note A.

may exist no trace of man. The substance which now shows itself in these present forms is ever agitated from below and from within; and not one form is permanent; not the earth, not man, not the soul. All came forth by unconscious and unintelligent development. All is moving on and passing away. The finite has no real existence. Man himself is but a transient phenomenon, — a shadow, — and all his works are dreams rather than realities. Before this world was evolved there was no personal agent to determine what should be; and now that it exists there is no reason why it should remain; no will orders its continuance, no intelligent power keeps it in being. There is not a form that hath permanency; there is nothing visible or invisible that can last. The material of yonder columns is fully as durable as your souls; the whole thing is but a passing show. All came forth out of darkness; all is drawn in perpetually and swallowed up. Everything perishes but the one substance; that does not perish, for that is God.

To revolt with horror from this appalling theory, to cry aloud against it, to stop the ear to its merciless, its diabolical utterances, this must surely be the course of every healthy mind. In its naked form, as now presented, it might be almost universally repelled and rejected. But I maintain that this is the system on which all the speculative infidelity of our age does actually rest, and that it contains the only logical explanation of the popular heresies touching the impersonality of the Divine Being. This consanguinity it will be my design in the next lecture to display so clearly that even the unlearned must recognize it. And, to approach the conclusion of the present remarks, let no one flatter himself with the idea that a system such as this could never attain a hold upon the public mind. Why might it not? What should restrain its growth were it not resisted and kept under by the word and sacramental power of the Holy Ghost? There are parts of the globe to-day wherein this system flourishes as the basis of the popular religion; and even here, where we hold high conceptions of our intelligence, there are writers and teachers whose thoughts are steeped in this poisonous compound, and who, notwithstanding, are esteemed and eulogized as the wisest and most judicious of men. But while we admit with shame that this is the case, we are glad to remember the history of the past and to observe how certainly the truth reasserts itself, though for the time depressed. Wherever they have thrown away the glorious faith in the living God and have lain them down in pantheistic dreams, the race has declined, men have fallen into degradation and intellectual torpor, and the way for the inevitable reaction has been prepared. In time the truth avenges itself. It did so memorably in the seventh century. About the year of our Lord 600, when the East lay sleeping and buried in the philosophic stupor, its limbs relaxed, its energies gone, on a sudden, and in the dead midnight, the avenger came. There arose in Arabia a man mighty in word and deed, whose mission seemed to be (and I doubt not that he had a mission) to revive that grand, that sacred truth, the personality and unity of God. Mohammed did not live in vain. Infidel though he was, impostor though he was, he yet spake truth when he denied the pantheistic lie, when he asserted a God creator of heaven and earth, when he affirmed that God alone is from eternity, that all things were made by His mind, His hand, His will, that He and His universe are in substance distinct. That was the creed of Mohammed. In that name the scimitars flashed to the light. In that name those scimitars swept the rank fields like the sickles through the standing grain. In that name his followers overran the East, the Persian empire and old Assyria, the African wilds, the far Cathay, the shores of Indus and the Ganges. It was but one word of truth against the brood, voluminous and interminable, of philosophy. One word of truth, but that word enough, the truth that God is God. Before the Saracens everything fell, simply because there was life in their creed, and because the countries that they overran were morally, intellectually, spiritually, physically dead. Before the Saracens everything fell. Everything, for a time, but not forever. Everything, till they were met, at the West, by the soldiers of the cross; by men who had a higher faith, a fuller knowledge, even the faith in the high and undivided Trinity, sublimest of all truths, the faith in Jesus Christ and Him crucified, grandest and most consoling of all that the mind of man hath received. There, against the cross-hilted swords of the good knights, was the scimitar broken. But elsewhere it did its work and well. Remember now for your comfort, that its main strength lay in its proclamation of one personal and living God to people who denied that personality and who confounded the Creator and His works. And I would ask, in conclusion, if this were the case when human agents alone were visibly engaged, — if the mere idea of the existence of such a being could so transform, strengthen, nerve the men who held it, — if the absence of that idea could so have demoralized and degraded the men who had lost it, — what should be the effect of the appearance among us of that very Being himself? He cometh now, He cometh at the last. Oh that it be not in burning wrath against the falsehoods of mankind! Oh that it be not in judgment, but in mercy! But be it as it may, cease we not our confession of Him as He is revealed unto us in the Church's Creed; and as for the theories of the schools of the day, let them be to us as the accursed thing wherein the children of the Lord will have no dealings whatever, lest they commit folly in Israel and be consumed at the last and awful account.

LECTURE III.

PANTHEISM IN ITS APPLICATIONS.

It was our object, in the preceding lecture, to present the system commonly known by the name of Pantheism, in its correct, scientific form. You are now aware that the word is not a mere vague term, nor one which may be loosely applied to almost any error against which the controversialist may desire to protest; but that it is the distinctive appellation of a theory as clear, as consistent, as intelligible as any that the mind of man or devil ever framed to hide the truth of God.

Having displayed the scheme in its crude form and in its technical expression, our next step must be to trace it in its practical applications. The system has a history of its own.* It is first encountered by the student when he investigates the Brahminism of India; and it formed the basis of the Egyptian and Chaldean religions, and of the philosophy of Greece. It was revived by the Alexandrine school, in the vain attempt to resist and oppose the advancing power of the faith of Jesus Christ. In the Middle Ages it again appeared;

* See Note B.

and after some preludes and preparatory motions, it burst forth once more, full formed, in the fifteenth and sixteenth centuries. In modern times it has been taught with assiduity by the French and German metaphysicians, who have accurately reproduced the principles of the ancient paganism; and from these new sources its leading ideas have been once more diffused throughout the province of human thought, in all their traditional antagonism to natural and revealed religion.

You must, therefore, observe that there has been in the world from very ancient times a vast metaphysical and historic doctrine, invented by men, and displacing the revelations made to them from time to time by our heavenly Father. Towards this scheme the mind naturally gravitates the instant it throws away the ideas of submission and obedience, and enters upon the path of free and licentious speculation.* This theory is now alive and active; and it forms the secret inspiration of the rationalistic systems of the day. We do not assert that it is held, to any considerable extent, in the shape in which it was exhibited in the preceding lecture. Few writers or speakers in this community would openly profess the pantheistic creed in the terms in which it has been formalized abroad. But we claim that the system has attained to an influence unsuspected by those who have not looked into this

* See Note C.

subject with attention. The historic, ethical, and psychological schemes of the "liberal" writers of the day have been framed alongside of this great heresy; and the popular idea of progress, apart from Christianity, and independent of religion and revelation, is but an application of its fatal principles. The doctrine of which we speak is everywhere and in everything. Its signs may be traced in quarters where the word "Pantheism" is repudiated. Its presence may be discovered in the very midst of those who know it not by name. Its secret workings are betrayed in speculations accounted harmless by the characteristic indifference of the day. If this be so, and if the age be full of pantheistic tendencies, if the metaphysical, moral, and social sciences be infected with them, though their maintainers and teachers ignore or conceal the fact, then must it be a matter of prime importance to trace the influence and operations of the system wherever they may be discerned, and to show how men may be tempted, seduced, tainted, poisoned by it almost at unawares.

But let me dwell for a moment on the fact that a system may exercise great power even where in its theoretic shape it is not understood. A man needs not to have an intelligent — or, so to express it, a philosophical — knowledge of a system, in order to be influenced or governed by it. Although quite ignorant of it, he may notwithstanding be wholly in its power. Much of our action, physical and moral, is involuntary action. Take, for example, Christians in general, how few there are who have a thorough and what we should call a scientific knowledge of all the articles of the Creed! It is not necessary that they should. The scientific knowledge of the faith is what we term the "Science of Theology." But theology is the study of a very limited number. It is not necessary that every Christian should be a theologian; it is neither necessary nor possible. To hold the Creed, to live thereafter, to be moulded by Church principles, to be thus fitted for heaven, all this may be without any scientific theological acquaintance with the dogmas of religion. Nor is this true alone of things ethical and spiritual; it is true of things physical as well. How little is ordinarily known of the science of common things! What a world of wisdom and wonder is there all about us, and yet how little is it understood! But such scientific acquaintance with the material world is, for the masses of the community, unnecessary and unattainable. A knowledge of the science of anatomy is not indispensable to enable one to walk. He who is ignorant of even the rudiments of physiology digests and breathes as well as the profoundest student of that branch of knowledge. The soldier fights well and wins the victory though he have no conception of the plan of the battle. But what is true of the good is just as true of the evil. What is true of Catholic theology is just as true of heresy. As, on the one hand, a man may guide his way by holy principles with which he has no formal acquaintance, and may beautifully exemplify in his life the power of a system which he would be utterly at a loss to comment on or to explain, so on the other hand may a man be holding and acting on principles subversive of revelation, while he is without a suspicion of their origin, their connections, their consequences. The very man who would revolt at the theory of Pantheism nakedly stated, may yet be holding the essentials of that system. He may be advocating pure pantheistic principles, though he knows nought of the scientific form of that monstrous scheme. Two things, therefore, are necessary: First, to see the thing itself just as it is, to discern its form and features, to visit the lair and to look at the monster in the remote retired places of its retreat; and secondly, to trace its footprints outside, to show where it has been and how it has wrought, though itself unseen, to convince men in a word that they may be its bond-slaves, though they have never looked on the face of their tyrant. The former of these necessary works was performed in the preceding lecture. To the latter will this present lecture be devoted.

What, then, are the offspring of this most repulsive parent? and what the brood which comes forth from this abominable womb? Let us consider.

The crime of Pantheism is this: that it removes God entirely from the scheme of the universe. It leaves no place, no work for God. It is a theory with which the idea of a personal, an intelligent, a living, thinking, speaking, acting God is wholly incompatible. Although it admit the terms "God" and "the Deity," yet it does so merely for convenience or as a concession to the popular belief. But the personal God, the eternal God, the creator, the ruler, the redeemer, the judge, the God who is infinitely distinct from his works, this God has no place in the pantheistic scheme.

The leading principles of the scheme are these:

Firstly, that the universe is substantially eternal.

Secondly, that things are what they are, not by creation, but by emanation and development.

Thirdly, that the order of events is not determined by a mind outside the world, but is a sequence from laws within it.

Fourthly, that all movement and advance and accession are from within and not from without.

It may therefore be stated as probable or certain that all propositions, all theories, all views which suppose or imply the absence of a personal God, and attach a quality of dignity, sufficiency, divinity, to finite things, are logically connected with the dark and hopeless system of which we are treating, and ought to be referred to it as to their genealogical tree. I propose to illustrate this proposition by reference to these six tendencies of our day.

Firstly, the tendency to assign to the world a very high antiquity.

Secondly, the tendency to make of history a fatuitous and fatal sequence of events.

Thirdly, the tendency to represent mankind as having been originally a set of barbarians but little if at all above the brutes.

Fourthly, the tendency to exalt the human reason above revelation.

Fifthly, the tendency to affect an ignorance about God.

And sixthly, the tendency to deny all and any objective truth.

There are many developments of Pantheism besides these, but to the consideration of these will our present remarks be limited.

And first. We often hear the Mosaic account of the creation impugned on the ground that the world must be much older than that account would seem to make it. We are told that the earth must have existed in its present state very much longer than the account in Genesis would lead us to suppose, and we are informed that there are grounds for assigning a very great antiquity to the human race. It is asserted that in ancient geological formations there have been found the remains of implements which must have been made by men, or bones which must have belonged to human beings; and that their presence in such positions proves the existence here on earth of men long before the times of Adam and

Eve. Now it is not designed to discuss these points, but simply to trace the relationship of particular views and opinions. And all these theories, — of the very great age of this globe, in its present form, of the very remote antiquity of the human race, — these we hold to be but tendencies toward the pantheistic position of the eternity of matter. Men do not like to say so; they would not admit it; but the appetency is that way. They long to get rid of the Mosaic history simply because it is the history of a creation by God. Indulge them in this desire, permit them to date back the origin of this present order of things, say sixty thousand years, and they will next insist on carrying it back six hundred thousand; they will look farther and farther backward for its origin toward the eternity which at length they would demand. Whenever you hear these views expressed, ascribe them to their proper place. To claim that the earth and man, as now existing, are of very great and vast antiquity, is hesitatingly to move towards the assertion that all matter and all substance are eternal. It is, to feel that way, to try you whether you will follow, to invite you toward the brink of that gulf. Such opinions are advanced, for the most part, by those who give themselves to scientific study, and neglect or decline to hear the word of God, by such as deal exclusively or mainly in physical science, by such as hold the modern forms of science to be completed and perfect, rather than what they are, conjectural shapes which another century's discoveries and growth may revolutionize and wholly change.

And secondly, you find persons at this day who would make of history a fortuitous or fatal sequence of events. This is of the essence of Pantheism. Whenever any one speaks of the history, whether of the world at large or of any particular tribe or family or nation, as if some finite agents controlled, some finite power directed it, you are ignorant, indeed, if you know not precisely what this means and implies. As, in the pantheistic scheme, there is no place for a Creator, so there is none for a Governor. "O Lord, our Governor, how excellent is Thy name in all the world!" This is the language of the Church. But such language cannot be uttered by philosophy. On the other hand, you hear such propositions as these: — that history is but the result of the development of the human mind; that the eras and epochs of history are times at which some idea prevails so powerfully as to rule and guide the course of affairs; that the careers of nations are but the steps and pathway of successive dominant thoughts; that at each epoch constitutions and governments, art and letters, religion and morals, are determined as to their quality or character by a common motive principle, the spirit of the age; that the development of the absolute essence, that eternal substance of which we spoke, is always taking increasingly perfect manifestations. The basis of these and all similar statements is one and the same,—the denial that God bears any active and intelligent part in the regulation and direction of the affairs of nations or men. He who makes that denial may perhaps acknowledge that a God exists. But what and who is a God who is nowhere efficiently, and who does and knows and sees nothing? It is a mere delusion. If you separate God from the historical course of this world, you thereby play into the hands of those who, in their impious theory, would remove Him not from history alone, but from the universe, and from our very thoughts. The idea that history is but a fatal sequence of events is an idea of Pantheism, and as near to it as a rib taken from its very side.

But thirdly, you will hear it often said that men in their original state were rude barbarians and grovelling degraded savages. It is asserted that the first men went on all-fours; that they had no intelligible language; that they lived on roots; that they were but a step above the beasts of the field: then that they advanced by degrees to their present state; that they invented language; that they formed themselves into society; that they arrived by degrees at the possession of laws, arts, religion. Now what does all this mean, and with what theory is it allied? With none save that theory of development which is part and parcel of the pantheistic scheme, and has no logical relation to any other philosophy under heaven. When you hear any one talk of a supposed original brute-like condition of mankind, — when you hear the assertion that language is the invention of man and not the gift of God to us, — when you hear of the successive acquirements of our race, and of their actual position as far superior to any enjoyed by them heretofore, — mistrust the speaker, or rather be sure that he too is anchored fast, though he perchance may not know it, to the pantheistic platform. For, according to that theory, there was no God to make man, no God to teach him, no God to enlighten him; therefore, he developed by degrees to what he is become. And back of all this miserable trifling about a primitive state of utter barbarism, and about a language of growls or grunts slowly working up to the fulness of such a system as the English tongue, — back of all this lie the less conspicuous but not worse downfalls of the doctrine that man was a brute before he became a man, and before that a fish, and before that a gluten, and before that an infusorial point. It is all part and parcel of one and the same falsehood, that things are what they are, not because God made them so, but because the eternal substance developed blindly into these forms. And that is the tenet of Pantheism.

In the fourth place, brethren, I call your attention to the evident vestiges and foot-tracks of this heresy in all that you hear so often and so boastfully said of the sufficiency of the human reason to itself, and of its power of independent and salutary action apart from the revelation of God. If there be no God whose mind made known to it shall constitute the law of human thought, then indeed must the reason be regarded as adequate to itself. But to say that it is thus adequate is to imply that there is no God. All, therefore, that we hear of the native powers of man, of the sufficiency of the human mind, of our ability to formalize all faith, all works, all belief, all duty, after our own will, all that men claim as a kind of royal prerogative and birthright in this behalf, smells of the system under discussion. Reflect, again, my hearers, that under that system there is really no God distinct from the common substance of which we all are parts; that the human mind is that substance, or a portion of it; that the human consciousness is that substance recognizing and comprehending itself. This tenet, although blasphemous, is in fact the real ground and source of all the high claims in behalf of the reason of man; it is associated with them, and they are affiliated with it. Why should we be bidden to rely upon our native powers alone, except that they who so exhort us doubt the existence of any other powers in which to rest? If there be no God, the reason *must* be sufficient to itself; and if you claim for it such sufficiency, you are practically denying the need of a God. I point you, therefore, to all these statements and to all these claims made and set up by men in the pride and naughtiness of their hearts, and affirm that however they may be smoothed over or toned down, or qualified for decency's sake, or through fear of pushing matters to extremes, there is underneath, notwithstanding, the same rank poison. No man can serve two masters. If you make of intellect a God, you dethrone the true God, and cast Him out. There is but one choice for the mind, — to submit to God, or to curse Him and die.

And fifthly, the presence of pantheistic error may be detected in another direction; as when any one is found affecting an ignorance of God, which he ascribes to the extreme difficulty of knowing Him. This sometimes sounds like a sheer affectation, and it seems to be fashionable and is thought to be impressive, especially among the poets. But there is something beneath. It is a solemn trifling with the hope of the world. In knowledge of God standeth our eternal life. In knowledge of Him and of His word modern civilization has been built up. What were man if he knew not God at all? And how much below his rightful place if he know Him but imperfectly? Therefore, to say that there is any supreme difficulty about knowing God, or learning of God, or coming to Him, is to imperil the very bond of all our strength, the very spring of all our hopes. Yet this is just what men do: affected men, conceited men, who stop their ears to His voice, and then complain that they can hear nothing; who turn their faces away, and then morbidly lament their misfortune in not enjoying the sight of Him. Distrust all this fashionable, this modern, this poetical cant (for you find it full often in our nineteenth-century poets) about the dimness of all the future and the dread uncertainties of our position, and the sadness of our lot in being forced to dwell with doubtfulness and uncertainty for our constant companions. Not half, not a quarter of this is genuine. In a Christian land like ours, in any land where there flourishes a branch of Christ's Church, there is no real difficulty in knowing God. We all know Him well enough for practical purposes. We all know Him well enough for our eternal salvation, and there are those who know Him too well for their soul's peace. Whenever you hear this disavowed, — whenever you hear loose, vague talk about God, as though it were next to impossible to satisfy one's self who He is, or what He is, or where He is, how He exists, how He has acted, or is acting now, whether He be or be not a person as we are persons, — then mistrust the words and look beneath for the scales, and the cloven feet, and the slime of the vast heresy of the ages. Pantheism has for her office to obscure all clearness of view, to destroy the power of lucid thought about the Deity, — making of Him, not a person, but an abstraction; not a being, but an influence or impression; not a reality, but a shadowy intangibility; not a Creator and Governor distinct from that world which He governs and created, but a kind of chemical base of the world; not a Lord upon the throne of the universe, but an all-pervading substance, without concentration, intelligence, power, force, or will. Such a God is utterly inconceivable, utterly unimaginable; a fleeting phantom to mock the weary sight, the stumbling foot, the empty hand. And the loose, discursive speech about the difficulty of knowing Him is true alone on the hypothesis that He is such a nonentity as has been described.

And sixthly, and finally, you may rest assured of the presence of pantheistic error in every case of denial of objective truth, of truth apart from him who holds it to be true. For there are those who tell us that all is true to him which any man thinks to be true. This is to say that the truth is in us, in our consciousness and in our thoughts. And there are those who say that every man may believe just as he chooses to believe, — as much, as little. This is to say that there is nothing which any of us ought to believe to his soul's health. Down these chasms the truth slides helplessly away, — for they are chasms, and below are spread the black, deep waters of the same heresy, the *limbus* of the lost, — for these denials of a truth outside of us, apart from us, independent of us, are based upon the assumption that all is one and the same substance, and that all things which we see are but transient and temporary modifications thereof. In face of such a principle no doctrine, no fact, no article of faith, could for one moment live. When men say that what any one thinks to be true is true for him; that for truth we must look within; that every one of us is, in his sphere, the judge of truth; that each man's mind shall dictate or determine his belief, and that each man's feelings do witness infallibly to his true condition; — when they say these things, they do but flatter with their lips and dissemble in their double heart. For it is to say, that there is no truth; nothing outside; all within. This is the pantheistic dogma. Nothing outside this world; nothing greater, wiser, better, nobler than the human mind; no evidence so good as internal evidence; no test of use against a man's deliberate convictions. And in such a scheme there can be nothing but truth; there can be no error and no falsehood, no wrong, no evil; all is good, and true, and right, and excellent; for all is God. I care not what schools of theology this may touch, what man's views it may impugn; but let it be affirmed, that he who says that you may repose secure in any Creed, if conscientious, — that you should rest, not in outward forms and agencies, but on inward feelings and conviction, — this man is playing into the hands of Pantheism, is helping on the work of those who would bind you and give you over to the monster, hand and foot.

Brethren, there is no proof that the earth in its present state has that high antiquity which the philosophers claim. And man was not at first a semi-brute; but God made him perfect, and saw the work that it was very good. And history is not a play of chance or fate, but a drama conducted by God in person. And God is not far off, and hard to know, but close to us and easy of access; nor hath He ever left Himself without a witness among His creatures. And the human mind is not sufficient to itself, but is without His revelation just where the eye is without light. And truth is not variable, but constant; not within us, but without, for us to make it ours, by reaching forth to it from out ourselves. And the Catholic religion, which thus corrects all falsehoods, is the only teacher under God whom we may safely follow; and the school of heresy, in which not merely the hard, gaunt theory is taught, but all its ingenious applications are made, that school is the council-room of confusion, and the entrance of ruin for the mind and soul and heart of all those who abide and continue therein.

LECTURE IV.

OBJECTIONS TO THE PANTHEISTIC THEORY.

In the previous lectures of this course I have endeavored, with what success yourselves must judge, to show the scheme of Pantheism, first, in its theoretic form, and secondly, in its practical applications. Such a division of the subject was rendered necessary by the fact that the system, in its unshorn deformity, is to be found only in the works of those scientific writers (especially of the French * and German schools) who logically carry out their principles and accept and avow the consequences, while it is commonly presented to us in the shape of dilutions more or less strong. Thus qualified and mitigated, however, it is encountered everywhere,— in theology, in philosophy, in history, in poetry, in the drama, and in the trashy literature of the day. To be able to recognize it in its disguised forms, one must know it in its natural shape; through such knowledge only can the identity between the theory and its applications be exhibited.

I now proceed, in continuation of this subject, to speak, first, of the way in which the Pantheists en-

* See Note D.

deavor to establish their conclusions; secondly, of the character of their alleged proofs; thirdly, of the objections which lie against the whole system in the consequences resulting therefrom.

And first, it is to be remarked that the Pantheist, in endeavoring to establish his principles, depends on certain definitions which he assumes to be correct, concerning the infinite and the finite, concerning substance and being. He also rests upon a very subtle system of the most abstract notions of metaphysics. All his philosophy is built on these primary definitions. My reference is chiefly to the speculative writers of the French and German schools. To endeavor to understand the language of their systems is an almost hopeless task, and yet it is evident that the main strength of those systems lies in this scientific jargon, and that they depend upon it for the success of their so-called demonstrations. But it is not from their positive methods only that the real position of these philosophers, relatively to the rest of mankind, may be inferred: nothing can be more significant than the care with which they avoid certain lines of argument to which we should expect a school aiming at wide influence to resort. For example, we never find one of these philosophers appealing to that grand old test, the common sense of men. We never discern in his writings a disposition to hear and abide by the verdict of the consent and concurrence of mankind. As to the traditional knowledge and faith of our race, he is dumb. To the received opinions, to the universal convictions of his fellow-beings, he dares not refer. All these directions he avoids with a sedulous care which cannot be mistaken, for he knows that these things are against him. The voice of common sense, the traditions that have come down through all time and among all nations, the convictions of the wise and pious all over the world, the facts of the existence of the visible Church of Christ, and the influence of the Holy Scriptures, —all these are against the Pantheist. He dares not face these witnesses; he cannot meet them on common ground. He invents his subtle system of metaphysics as a necessity of his position, because a special and peculiar set of arms, offensive and defensive, is required by the man who is to appear in conflict with history, and testimony, and consent, and experience, and the judgment and common sense of all our race. His battle is against the mind, the logic, the intelligence, the heart, the soul, of the universal human family.

To speak, in the second place, though briefly, of the character of these alleged proofs. Already laboring, from the very first, under the disadvantage of contradiction by every reliable voice to which an appeal can reasonably be made, they stand convicted of weakness in this behalf, — that they are arbitrary in themselves, and therefore powerless in result. Each science has its language. But the science of Pantheism is a mere speculative cloud. It has its language and its proper terms, and in them lies its strength. Yet no man need admit the exactness of its definitions, nor is it possible for the masters of this science to show cause why the world should accept the peculiar nomenclature which they employ. Unless this be done, however, the argument which lives in those special definitions must fail. The characteristic language of the school respecting substance, personality, unity, the finite and the infinite, matter, spirit, soul, truth, certitude, and the like, we Christians may reject; and we may demand that the terms to be used in all questions touching the existence and nature of the Almighty, the being and powers of man, and similar topics, shall be such terms as have been familiarly known and used in the Church, and may be understood of ordinary minds. We may require, as a preliminary, that this unintelligible jargon of the Rationalists shall cease, and that, in subjects eminently practical, we shall be permitted to know just what these teachers mean and whither they would lead us. If this be done, the power of the system is broken. Opposed by common sense, ignoring the realities of our situation, admitting no fact as historic, explaining no mystery, leaving behind it difficulties more formidable than those of which it complained and which it proposed to remove, the tongue of this philosophy ceases, and the knowledge thereof vanishes away.

I proceed to speak, thirdly, of the objections to this philosophy in respect to the consequences which it involves. And since this is by far the most important branch of the subject, it is to its full treatment that the remainder of this lecture will be devoted.

The first consequence from the Pantheistic philosophy to which I shall advert is this: that, according to its principles, the world and man do of necessity exist, and that they are part of God Himself. From eternity has there been this so-called universal substance. But the being which is from eternity is not contingent and relative, but absolute and necessary. The world, however, is but that substance realized in certain visible forms, and man is that substance arrived at its highest manifestation thus far; and therefore the world and man have, as to their substance, a necessary existence. Again, that substance, in its entirety, is God, and the world and man are parts of that substance, and therefore the world and man do not merely exist of necessity, but the world and man are parts of God. As to this conclusion, Pantheism hesitates not to avow it; nay, it glories in it as its most valuable discovery; and that blasphemous idea, at which the Christian shudders, is the first of the inestimable boons bestowed by this infidel philosophy on mankind.

But, secondly, it follows not less clearly, from the principles now under consideration, that God is absolutely dependent on the world, and absolutely dependent upon man. We have been trained in the Church to think of God as the sovereign Lord of all; but the God of Pantheism is weak, and speechless, and unconscious, and powerless, without the universe and without us. For consider, brethren, that, according to this philosophy, the eternal substance has in itself no shape, no mind, no will, no sight, no consciousness; it attains to these in developing upward, and in taking the successive forms of the universe. Until it thundered, God had no voice. Until there were mountains and hills, and suns and moons and stars, God had no definite life. Until there were planetary orbits, God had no orderly motion. Until there were brutes, God had no instincts, no desires, no feeling. Until there were men, God had no consciousness, no perception of Himself, no will, no thought. Thus He depends on us. It is He who lives in us, rather than we in Him. Without the universe, without what we mistakingly call His works, He is quite imperfect and incomplete; for it is only through the universe that this poor, blind, unformed, anomalous being can express itself or assert itself. This conclusion inevitably follows from the principles of the system; and this degraded and emasculted conception is that which Pantheism, with ghastly leer, offers us as a substitute for the Father, the Redeemer, the Governor, in whom thus far the world has trusted itself, and on whom we suppose that we depend.

And thirdly, it is a consequence of this philosophic theory that it obliterates those distinctions on the existence and realization of which all social, moral, and intellectual life and progress depend. There is, according to the Pantheistic tenet, no distinction at all between the finite and the infinite, all things that we see and perceive and know being but parts of the one infinite and universal substance. But to maintain this principle, to say, as they do whose views we are now examining, that the finite has no true and separate existence of its own apart from the infinite, is to kill the finite by this tremendous, this fatal juxtaposition. It results from this idea, (to look to that which most nearly concerns ourselves,) that men have no real existence of their own, that we are but phantoms, that our acts are but imaginary, that our lives (as we call them) are but dreams; for we are parts or fragments of that ever-developing infinite, that ever-progressing infinite, which alone has any and all reality. And thus, in like manner, the Pantheistic theory destroys effectually all distinction between the human reason and the divine, all distinction between the life of creatures and the life of God. All boundary lines are swept away, all differences disappear, all life, all thought, all reason, all existence, are struck and heaped and massed together in one monstrous lump, one inconceivable aggregate. There is a complete identification, or, which is the same thing, there remains but one appalling chaos.

And fourthly, you perceive, brethren, that in this system the Personal God disappears utterly from view. That grand and beneficent figure, the form of the Father of all, is dethroned. As we comprehend the sacred term, there is left no God. A substance, impersonal, there is; but we cannot imagine that unintelligible, unreasoning, unthinking, unloving state of impotence as our Father, our Creator, our Redeemer, our Sanctifier, our Friend. The God in whom we have believed is gone. In the following lecture of this course it is proposed to state, (and how refreshing will be the task after this wading through the Pantheistic slough!) the full, the true, the dear, the blessed conception of the Almighty which we have received in the Church and find in the sacred Scriptures. Let it be sufficient here to remark that such a conception, in connection with the system whose tenets are an identity of substance throughout the universe and a principle of spontaneous development as the only law of life and progress, is merely and absolutely impossible. The God of Pantheism is not a person, exists not personally, has no personal attributes; it is merely a kind of substratum on which everything is founded, a kind of material out of which everything is built, a kind of great sum total of all things, an enormous vortex in which its own concretions whirl round and round forever. Oh, what a black and damnable outrage is that which Pantheism attempts to perpetrate!

It would rob the creation of its Maker, the world of its Governor, time of its Providential Arbiter, man of his Father and Friend! What greater crime than to try this gigantic fraud and to leave us nothing in His place?

Ah, brethren, those last words were not correct. Pantheism does *not* leave us destitute. It takes away God, but it does *not* leave His place empty. Had it done so, our charge against it were not so heavy and the wrong were less; for that is what Atheism does, and therefore Atheism is less to be feared. For Atheism, denying that there is any God, and not undertaking to fill the place which it has thus proclaimed to be vacant, leaves behind it a void, the void of that negation, a void which cries out to be filled, which calls to its object, which craves incessantly in the torments of hungry despair. The void which Atheism thus makes in the universe protests against the process by which it was formed; it cries aloud; accuses the folly of the man who hath said there is no God; it denies the very denial, and leaves the victim no refuge but in an utter brutalization, in a completed degradation from which he must escape, and from which he cannot escape save by coming back to faith. But Pantheism eschews that error. Pantheism is the last device of the devil, and by far the subtlest. Atheism is simple and blunt; but Pantheism is crafty and sly. Atheism is honest in its way, and by its very honesty defeats its end. But Pantheism profits by observation of the error of its predecessor. It strikes out God from the universe; but it leaves no void,—no void to ache and protest and demand mercy. It fills the void with a calculating coolness; it fills it by deifying the world and man.

This is our fifth allegation against the system: that it confounds God and the universe in such a way as to make of them but one. That it confounds God and man, the divine nature and the human, in such wise as to identify them. It dethrones God, but not so as to leave His throne empty. It dethrones God, but it sets up man in His place. "He, as God, sitteth in the temple of God, showing himself that he is God." It transports the divine personality into man; it affirms that in man God hath consciousness, affection, will, personal existence. It subjects and satisfies the idea of the greatness, the majesty, the worthiness of man; it makes of him the real, the only deity: and thus the void is filled by the sovereign pride, the endless ambition, the supreme self-confidence of the human heart. This thing is worse by far than aught that Atheism ever attempted. It is crafty, it is malignant, it is immense in audacity; and yet it is literally the very thing which the Pantheists have done, the last and highest conclusion of their approved writers, in whose printed works may these atrocious blasphemies be found, line upon line, and statement upon statement, until the very hairs of our head should stand on end as we read.

Think then, brethren, in the sixth place, of the bearings of this view on certain questions vital to us as a race. There follows, as a consequence, the reduction of certainty to uncertainty throughout the province of thought; the obliteration of all distinction between good and evil, between right and wrong, between virtue and vice, in the sphere of morality; for according to the Pantheistic scheme there is no divine mind, no divine thought, until the infinite and universal substance has developed up to man. In man, therefore, that substance first has consciousness; in man that substance first thinks. But that substance is God; therefore the thought of man is the thought of God, the mind of man the mind of God, the speech, the voice of man, are the speech and voice of God. Now what does all this mean? This, and no less, — that all the thoughts of any individual mind are divine thoughts; that all the imaginings, the opinions, the views of any mind, of every mind, are divine; that every wish of your heart, that every appetite of your soul, that every consideration of your intelligent understanding are together and alike divine. But, you will say, men do not think alike, do not judge alike, do not desire alike. It is so. And thus all ideas of any fixed and settled permanent quality in thought are lost. It follows that there can be no such thing as absolute and immutable truth: all truth is mobile and progressive; all thoughts are right and true in their way. No thought of any human mind can be wrong: it may be incomplete, but that is all; and as the idea of an absolute and unchanging truth independent of our minds is thus removed, so there doth perish in like manner to its merest vestiges the idea of a moral law, and of a distinction between right and wrong, good and evil, vice and virtue. For if man be God thinking and acting, then, as all man's thoughts are divine, so must be his acts: pride, pleasure, passion, cruelty, ambition, lust, are but the necessary development of moral tendencies in the original substance. That substance, though it have no personality, is supposed to have and to hold all possible, all conceivable tendencies within itself, and these are developed and evolved in human thought, in human desire. All our thoughts are divine thoughts, all our desires are divine desires. This is what the New England transcendentalists have meant all along, in using the pernicious language, that what we call error is only incomplete truth, and that what we call evil is only incomplete good,—which means, at bottom, that there is no such thing as an absolute good and evil, an absolute right and wrong. In New England they are cautious what they say and how they express themselves; but the Pantheists abroad are more straightforward. They stick not at the last conclusion, from the mere expression of which one shrinks appalled; but it must be said, it shall be said, to let you look for once over the edge and far down into the deep, — they have affirmed that the development of man is the development of God too; that as the primal substance is advancing it is God who advances; that He, far from being unchangeable, is always improving and going forward to what He was not before; * that we cannot conjecture what God may become; that whatsoever appears to be evil is only in appearance evil, but, in reality, imperfect good; that whatever appears to be error is not really error, but only imperfect truth; and since all, in thought or act, which we call error, evil, vice, is but part of the one grand and perpetual progression and development, therefore that God is not merely good, truth, and virtue, but that He is error, vice, and evil! So wrote a pantheistic philosopher in France; † and when he penned those words and spoke them abroad, if there be ears and eyes in hell to hear and see, that place must have rung with applause, and shouts of approval must have stormed round all the sides of the infernal pit.

And, brethren, I will detain you with but one more of these pictured consequences of this message and burden of woe and death. It is the pantheistic view of history, — of the history of the ages and of nations and of men. History, according to these writers, is not ordered by God; nations are not

* See Note E.

† Proudhon: *Système des Contradictions Économiques.*

ruled by God; individual life is not overlooked by God: but history is merely the continued development of humanity. It is supposed by this philosophy to be divided into epochs. Each of those epochs is regarded as a time of the domination of some one element of the mind. Nations are the representatives of ideas, and it is the mission of each nation to manifest the special idea with which its existence is allied; therefore the part which each nation is to play is fixed by a prior necessity, by an absolute fate. The idea to be represented by each nation has connection with the part of the globe which the nation occupies, — with climate, physical circumstances, temperature, — with commercial advantages, with natural resources, with the productions of the soil. The pantheistic Philosophy supposes two things (in its applications to the history of the world): first, a law of progress which is not the will of God, but an inflexible and inevitable necessity of sequence; and secondly, a necessary and absolute inspiration in humanity. The ideas of which we have spoken are all, in their way, divine; divine, but incomplete. They are developed one by one. Each, being but a partial view of truth, must, in its turn, yield and disappear. History is the record of these mutations and transitions, as embodied in the nations of the earth; but at all times and in every age, constitutions, governments, arts, sciences, religion, have but one common root, "the spirit of the age." There can be no such thing as national crimes, as national injustice, as national wrong. The whole development is good. Through war, rebellion, revolution, — through oppression and tyranny and misgovernment, — through empire, kingdom, democracy, — it is all good, it is all well. Call nothing a crime if it accords with the spirit of the age. Count nothing a virtue if it departs from the spirit of the age. Away with the unmeaning terms of law, order, justice, liberty, right, wrong, national honor and glory, national shame and reproach. These are but empty names; for all is but one progression, one development of the infinite substance, and the shadow which you call a nation is as hollow as the spectre which you call a hero, a patriot, a traitor, a demi-god. Nations represent ideas; and when the idea has been expressed, the part of the nation is played. And great men are the priests and missionaries of ideas, and their careers are valuable for study only in that respect. But all moral distinctions, whether as to the nation's course or the individual's character, are futile and vain. It is but the march of a great spirit, — the spirit of the age.

Here let us pause and draw a long breath of relief, and stop; for the work which was proposed is done so far as its first object extends. Enough has been said of this dreadful heresy. Hereafter we shall be refreshed by the consolations of the Gospel, and by the blessed message concerning the "One

God and Father of all," the "One Lord Jesus Christ," the Holy Ghost, the Lord and the Life-giver, whom we know in the peaceful ways of the faith. Referring, therefore, to the next evening the examination of the truth, let us, finally, turn the fatal page of the Philosophy of this world and leave its sentences to their proper dust and darkness, with thanksgiving unto Him who hath delivered us and the human race out of the power of that darkness, and hath translated us into the kingdom of His dear Son.

LECTURE V.

THE CHRISTIAN IDEA OF ALMIGHTY GOD.

THE time has arrived at which the character of these lectures must be changed, and none can be so glad of this as he who has undertaken to prepare them. It might indeed appear as though some apology were due for having led you so far and so long in the paths of an heretical labyrinth, perhaps more cunningly contrived than any other that Satan ever made to ensnare and destroy the human soul. But still it was necessary to show the disease in full; to probe the wound far down; to trace, as we have done, the whole pantheistic malady, first in its real nature, and then in some of its more evident symptoms; to follow it out to its consequences; and to bring to the light its last and ruinous results. But that portion of our work is done. The pantheistic conception of God has been distinctly presented; that parody of truth, that destroyer of our hope, that contradiction of every positive statement, of every assured conviction, has been laid before you in the immobility of its fatalism, in the rigidness of its monotonous despair. From that dark specimen of intellectual aberration may we now right gladly turn, betaking us to our home in the Church of God, reading in her sacred books the word of truth, and contrasting the Almighty as He really is with this void and irrational phantom to which a false philosophy has dared to apply His sacred name.

"*I believe in one God, the Father Almighty, Maker of heaven and earth, and of all things visible and invisible.*" In this sublime affirmation does the Church begin to teach us what to think of the Lord Most High.

When the Church thus speaks to us of Almighty God, she speaks : —

First, of One who hath a proper personal existence.

Secondly, of One who is distinct from the works of His hands.

Thirdly, of One who is most closely connected with the world.

And fourthly, of One who cannot vary or change.

These are her declarations as against the pantheistic scheme; and it will be the object of this lecture to develop each of these statements in order, and to show, as far as the limited time will allow, what each one of them implies.

And first, Almighty God is one who hath, eternally and essentially, a full, a real, a proper personal existence. You all know, brethren, though some of you might be at a loss to define in scientific mode, what is meant by a person. You all know what is intended when we speak of persons as contradistinguished from things. You all know that a stone or a tree is not a person ; and that a man or a woman or a child is. Now, whatever you understand to be expressed, or whatever plain, simple-minded folk commonly understand to be expressed, by the term "a personal existence," such an existence has Almighty God. Only that in Him personality must have a perfection which it never could have in creatures ; because He is every way so incomparably greater and better than they. Your dictionaries will tell you, if you refer to them, that personality is constituted by certain capacities, and particularly by the power of conscious thought. A thinking, intelligent being; a being who can contrive and direct; who acts knowingly and understandingly ; — that is a person. These brief, popular definitions are sufficient for our purpose, without entering into the profounder explanations which theology and philosophy afford. But observe, that if to think, to perceive, to have intelligence, to enjoy and use the power of conscious thought, — if this be to have personality, — then when we say that Almighty God is a person, we mean that He is one who thinks and knows and perceives, not merely as we do, but far more perfectly in every respect ; who has consciousness, but a consciousness so full that ours compared to His is less than the vague perception of infancy as compared to the luminous vision of manhood ;

who thinks, but with a power and range and scope of thought so great that our thoughts are, in comparison to His, what folly is to wisdom; who has, forever and essentially, every personal quality and attribute which we can trace in ourselves, and by which we establish our difference from mere inanimate things, but in infinite perfection. Personality has many degrees. The lower a creature may be, or the higher, in the scale of life, the narrower, or the fuller will be the attribute in question. A stone, a tree, a hill, a river, the clouds, the elements, the mechanical and chemical forces, — these are in no sense personal beings. But all animals have personality; all that have the power of motion, together with a will; all that are conscious of pleasure, of pain, of want; all that have a logical faculty: all these are persons. Above the rest stands man, — above and far beyond the rest in this endowment. But God is greater still. In Him this quality of personal existence is found in final and supreme perfection. Settle it in your minds what you will understand by the term, and then add to it an infinity of excellence: God is all that you have thought of, and infinitely more.

And, secondly, Almighty God, as Christianity proclaims Him, is one who is distinct from all the works of His hands. In His substance He is eternal; and there is no eternal substance besides. And not at any time, or in any manner, hath aught of that divine and eternal substance been communicated to any creature. It cannot be shared with creatures. It cannot be parted among creatures. It cannot flow away into works or forms. It is the indivisible, the inseparable, the essential nature and substance of Almighty God. He cannot be divided, nor cut up into parts, nor transformed, now into one shape, and anon into another; for He is from eternity to eternity the same. He made all things. But He made nothing out of His own substance as out of a material; to assert that would be sheer blasphemy. He made, at first, and by His omnipotent word brought into being, a material which had no existence before; this He created before aught else, and of this He made and framed the worlds. But that substance, that building-material, was not Himself. It was brought into being in time, by Him who is eternal. It was not, in any wise, until He caused it to be. And thus the universe, which was made of material not previously existing, is infinitely distinct from God. No part of His substance hath ever passed over, or flowed into, or become amalgamated with the world, or with any portion thereof. There is not, as Pantheism says, one universal substance. The substance of things created is finite, limited, temporary, contingent, variable; the infinite and eternal substance is, in one word, God. There it is that Pantheism and Christianity part. The philosophic system confounds God and nature. The holy faith divides them by the difference of infinity.*

The old philosophers agreed not together as to the manner in which God and the world were one. It will repay us to consider, in passing, their wild theories; for the statement of those theories will bring more clearly to light the Catholic faith. They all held the view that God and the world were of one and the same substance; but they had four different forms of the common theory, and they used the words generation, emanation, limitation, and animation, as descriptive terms to mark the different shades of their thoughts. Some of them said that God made the world out of His own substance, as the parent begets the child of his own blood; and this was the theory of generation. Others again supposed that all the creation has come forth from God, just as light from the sun, or heat from flame, or vapor from water; and this was the theory of emanation. A third class considered that visible objects are but a modification, or a series of modifications, of a substance which never changes; and they held that the universe is made of God, just as seas, gulfs, bays, and straits are formed of the same vast ocean, in the indentations of enclosing shores; and this was the theory of limitation. And, finally, there were those who thought that God was inside of the universe and mixed up with it, a kind of

* See Note F.

soul, making everything alive and keeping it fresh and sound, as the soul preserves the body in man; and this was the theory of animation.

But all these views are false together, for one and the same falsehood lies in them all, and back of them all, — that falsehood about the identity of substance.* Which falsehood is met in the statement of the Catholic faith, that God and the works of God are infinitely distinct. They are not the same. He is not a part of the universe; nor is the universe a part of Him. He made all things; but that wherewith He wrought, and whereof He made them, was not before: it was created; it was not eternal. None is eternal but He; and no substance is eternal but His. And since the world is not eternal, therefore it was not of His substance that the world was made.

But in our holy religion, beloved brethren, there is nothing one-sided, nothing incomplete. The mind of the Church, as shown in her Creed and confessions, is large and wide as the mind of the Spirit and of the Holy Ghost. And, therefore, while we are taught that Almighty God is infinitely distinct from the universe, we must at the same time hold fast the truth that He is most closely, most intimately connected with it. For these articles of our faith do act towards each other unto compensation; either would be unsatisfying without the other, while

* See Note G.

both together leave nothing to be desired. Almighty God is not distant from that world which He has been pleased to call into being; on the contrary, He is exceeding near. Nowhere is He the same as the world; yet nowhere is He absent from it. These two are essential truths. There can be no religion, in the proper sense of the term, where they are not confessed. His entire distinction from the universe, and His closest union with it, — of these two points must men be convinced, as indispensable conditions to true belief and healthful thought.

But how shall we harmonize statements which appear to conflict? By referring one of them to the divine substance, and the other to the divine personality. As to His nature, Almighty God is infinitely distinct from the works of His hands; but as to His personal attributes, He is inseparably united to them. In His power, in His vision, in His will, in His thought, in His sympathies, in His love, He is nowhere far off, he is never absent. No occurrence can take place without His knowledge. No creature can exist but by His command. No point in all the universe can, though but for an instant, be hidden from His sight. He knows all, He sees all, He thinks of all, He feels for all, He loves all. He is everywhere, as to His thought, His power, His goodness. And yet, nowhere is there the least approach to confusion or commingling of substance. These are the two grand truths on which our whole religion is built, and in which all our hopes reside. You cannot deny either without risking the loss of all that we have most precious. For to deny the former, and to say that God and the universe are *not* absolutely distinct, as to essence and substance, is to admit the pantheistic tenet of unity of substance, with all the woe, and all the horror, and all the hopelessness which we have seen to result from that monstrous assumption. While, on the other hand, to deny the second article of the faith, and to say that God and the world are not most intimately connected, is to reject the sweet truth that we have a Father in heaven, and the consolatory assurance that a wise and thoughtful Providence overrules the course of affairs; it is to separate God from His creation and from man; it is to suppose in Him a being without sympathy and without care; to regard the world as a system blindly led along by fate or chance or unimpassioned law; to consider the human race as beings without a father, a governor, a guide, without a redeemer, a preserver, a ruler; as having no one to pray to, and no one to trust to, and no one to account to, nor any to encourage, to sustain, to reward. These are the results of denial of either of those cardinal truths; Pantheism threatens on the one side, Atheism on the other. And, to avoid those extremes, we must, from the heart, embrace, and ever hold fast, and ever firmly profess, the two sister truths, that Almighty God, as to His eternal,

His essential, His incommunicable substance, is infinitely and absolutely distinct from His creation and from the whole frame of the vast universe; and that the same Almighty God, as to His personal life, His power, His will, His thought, His love, His providence, His knowledge, His vision, is everywhere present, and everywhere most intimately connected with that same creation, with every creature, and with everything, and with every part of that same universe. These two affirmations are the columns which hold up the sacred temple of the faith. Take either of them away, and the edifice topples to its utter destruction; and if it so go down, it must drag the whole social system into the chasm.

There remains but one more of those statements, to the unfolding of which this lecture was set apart. Fourthly, therefore, Almighty God must be thought of by us as a being who cannot alter or change. You remember what horrid blasphemy the pantheist has uttered in respect of progress, and development, and improvement in God, meaning, by God, that eternal substance of which he wildly dreams. But the God of Christianity and of the gospel is not that image which the philosophers have set up. He is one in whom there can be no variableness, neither shadow of turning. From eternity to eternity He abides the same. God is the same in two respects: first, as regards His essential being, in which no alteration can occur; and secondly, as regards our thoughts and conceptions of Him, which cannot in the least degree affect His positive reality. In declaring that unchangeableness, therefore, we intend that double reference; we mean to say, not only that He is evermore the same God, yesterday, and to-day, and forever, but also, that His independence of any cogitations of ours concerning Him could by no possibility be more complete. All this is expressed in that sublimest name that ever was uttered or conceived, that name which He announced as His own, *Ego sum qui sum:* "*I am that I am.*" What marvellous power, what inflexibility of strength, what calm majesty in that title: "I am that I am!" The same, the unchanging, the Lord, from age to age. Not, "I am whatsoever you think me to be;" not, "I am this to one man and that to another;" not, "I am to you whatever you prefer that I should be, whatever you, as you follow your self-willed thoughts, consider that I ought to be, and feel confident that I must be; but, I am that I am! I am He that was from eternity, and is now, and is to come. I am He that hath no dependence on the world, nor any need of man; that taketh not counsel of creatures, neither hath learned from them the path of judgment. I am the first and the last. The Creator. The Father. The Provident Ruler. The Maker of man, the Redeemer of man, the Sanctifier of man. Your Lord, your Rewarder, your Judge. O children of men, what avail your thoughts that ye should think by them to affect the absolute truth of My being? How can ye dream this wild thing, that I should change with any and with every imagination of your minds concerning Me? Can there be named in all the range of human delusions one so huge as this, that any man should suppose that God is whatever he imagines God to be? Can there be told, of all the duties of man, one more necessary than this, that he hold fast his belief in the absolute perfection, in the entire self-sufficiency, of his Creator? I am that I am. Judge not of Me by any rule of your own, but judge by what I have declared. Hear not men, but listen to My eternal word. My Son, the only begotten, He hath declared Me. Hear ye Him. For He only hath the words of life. Learn of Him My great and glorious name,—the name of one who is immutable, unalterable, beyond the reach of any and all agencies, in the perfection of My eternal state and nature."

Thus, beloved brethren, has the attempt been made to set forth to you the Christian idea of God; or rather, to speak of God, not as men have thought Him to be, but as in truth He is. You have heard the declarations of the Church to all mankind, in this behalf:—

First, that He is really a personal being, like ourselves.

Secondly, that He is in no way confused or commingled with the works of His hands, but infinitely distinct from them.

Thirdly, that He is most intimately connected with the world and with all its inhabitants, with all that therein is.

Fourthly, that He is what He is, positively and absolutely, whatever our views or opinions concerning Him may be.

Take these first principles of our holy religion as tests, amid the vagueness of modern thought. Make these great truths the starting-point of your faith, and the boundaries of every imagination of your spirits concerning the Most High. When you are presented with the theory of a God who has evidently been fashioned and shaped by the subtle wit of man to suit its own preconceptions, know that this idea is a mere idol, and reject and denounce it as a travesty of that high and lofty One whose sublime existence is independent of aught beyond itself. When you hear men talk of a God who cares not for this world, nor for us, nor for our affairs, — of a God who is supposed to have resigned to arbitrary and unthinking law the order and direction of the course of this world, — reject that low conception as an utter misrepresentation, as a shameless parody of Him by whom the very hairs of our heads are all numbered; without whom not even a sparrow falleth to the ground; whose eye, whose love, whose providence, whose power, are everywhere, searching the darkness and the light, and never failing, in any instant of time, nor at any point of the immeasurable universe. As for a God who is substantially one with his creatures; or who dwells afar, careless of our concerns; or who is destitute of thought, or sight, or consciousness; who can work no miracle, who can speak no word to our bodily ears, who cannot show Himself to our bodily vision: there is no such being, save in the brains of the deceiver and the deceived. The real God is indeed a reality; the God with whom we have to do is not a creature of our minds, but the sovereign Lord of heaven and earth. It is He that made the world and all things therein; who giveth to all life and breath and all things; who hath made of one blood all nations of men for to dwell on all the face of the earth, and hath determined the times before appointed and the bounds of their habitations; who is not far from every one of us. This is the God whom Paul preached, when he stood on Mars' Hill, face to face with the epicureans and the stoics of ancient time. This is the God whom we must preach face to face with the spiritualists, the transcendentalists, the philosophers of modern days. Nor doubt the triumph of the faith in Him. Though these false priests build up their altar of abomination, and fashion their god and set him up thereon; though they substitute the worship of a rationalistic deity for the old, the only hope of all the ends of the earth; though they cry from morning even till noon, "O Baal, hear us!" though antichrist be thus revealed as the latter days come nigh; and though this false deity at length appear sitting in the temple of God, and showing himself that he is God, even in the temple of the deluded heart and mind which deifies its own opinion and bows before it: yet wait, brethren, till the time of the evening sacrifice, till the altars be rebuilt, till the true God appear in glory for the salvation of His people; and then the dream shall be over and the spell broken, and there shall be heard a sound, as it were the voice of great multitudes and of many waters; and as that awful sound takes shape and volume, it shall ascend far to the pealing dome above, proclaiming, "The Lord, He is the God! The Lord, He is the God!"

LECTURE VI.

THE CHRISTIAN FAITH IN ITS APPLICATIONS.

In the preceding lecture there was set forth, though briefly and imperfectly, the true Catholic faith concerning the existence and attributes of Almighty God. It now remains to draw our remarks to a close. We have passed together through those places in which, as in a synagogue of Satan, strange doctrines are taught; we have heard the sound of other systems ; we have measured the length of their separation from the everlasting truth, and have gauged the depth of that abyss into which they are capable of casting down the mind of him who yields to their solicitations. Emerging at length from those forbidding regions of profane speculation, we have considered in a general way, and with a view to comparison, the leading principles of the Christian faith concerning Almighty God. It is now proposed, by way of a suitable conclusion of the work, to dwell upon the idea of Him as that idea is presented to us in the Church, and to show its practical application in the order of our daily life.

How clear is that idea, and how full ! how plain

and accessible to the grasp of faith! how capable of meeting all spiritual requirement and necessity! A home-like presence, a familiar neighborhood, a close and true and real relationship. "What shall a man give in exchange for his soul?" saith the Lord. But of Him, and of the Father, may we exclaim, using and applying His words, "What shall a man give in exchange for his God?" Surely, if bereaved of our simple faith in God, — the Father, the Son, the Holy Ghost, — we could never rest content with any of those loose and vague conceptions to which the holy name has been applied. The phantom raised by Philosophy, the shadow evoked by that witchcraft of the subtle understanding, by that magic of the godless imagination, — this phantom, this shadow, is not that in which we have trusted, nor is it He whom we do know.

Perhaps the readiest way of learning how precious, how satisfying is the idea of God, as He hath revealed Himself to us through the Gospel, would be to reflect how much and what we should lose if that idea were lost, — how much of our daily life must go, if that idea were gone.

Imagine, therefore, a state of things which may perhaps arrive before the end of the world; and suppose that the belief in the Holy Trinity, the God of Christianity, had become, for the most part, extinct in the breasts of men. And suppose that in its place there had become established (if aught so shapeless and anomalous can be spoken of as established) the theory of a Universal-Substance-Deity, and the idea of a self-development in that substance as the only mode of life and advance, and as the only assignable reason or explanation of things as they occur and are. And, furthermore, suppose some man, who should be the survivor from a former age of faith, — one who had believed once, but afterwards resigned and renounced his earlier thoughts,—a man who, once a Christian, had outlived his better days, to stand at last avowed a philosophizer and a rationalist. To what should such a man look back? And, as comparing his former with his later self, what should he have lost, and to what extent would his intelligent and conscious existence have been affected by the change? Let us reflect.

And first, to speak of his personal and individual life. From that sphere all idea of a Father, a Protector, a Guide, a Friend, would have utterly faded away. The God of Pantheism is not a Providence over us: it has no thought, no heart, no love, no power. All those conceptions, therefore, in respect to the Deity, would have become extinct in the mind of the man whose case we are considering. In the morning light, as he opened his eyes to it, there would be no sign of a Divine Protection, renewing the days of his life; and though the sun arose never so brightly in the splendors of the east, there would be no logical ground for thankfulness towards any Ruler of the Universe, for the gift of that warm and clear shining. So, too, the song of nature, reviving at the dawn and in the beams of the new day, must be no longer interpreted as if it were a hymn of praise; but the crowing of the cock, the matins of birds, the hum of joyous life, all breaking forth together in full concert, must be accounted but a series of fatalistic occurrences, and not the response of a glad creation to that beneficent Creator from whom it all hath birth. Our Father would have been banished from the dawn and early morning hour, and what was once, and is now, to Christian ears, a cheerful anthem of praise in which it becomes man to bear his part by devotion, thanksgiving, and prayer, would change to a medley of sounds, without a purpose and without an object. But again: this philosopher-religionist must go forth to the duties of the day, — nay, not to the *duties*, there can be no such thing, for where there is no relationship there can be no duty, — he must go forth to his work, with no sense of One who shall work with him; with no invocation of a blessing from any quarter, for there can be no blessing where there is none to speak it. And so, through the twelve hours of the day, he would pursue his course, so far as any power above him might be regarded, alone. No eye to watch, no ear to hear, no hand to show the path; not one in heaven to care for, to mark, to approve, to regard. To his view those heavens must be utterly empty: no angels there, no throne high and lifted up, no paradise, no happy souls in light; nought but a great concavity of self-forming, self-developing material, cold as the ice, pitiless as winter, empty as his own heart. Thus going through the day in solitude, he is overtaken at last by the fall of night; and the night, so falling on that barren day, is the fit and true symbol of the darkness of a universe without a God distinct from itself.

Such must be, to the man whose position we are tracing in imagination, the experience of any common day of his life, when days run smoothly by. But days do not always keep that even, measured beat. There are emergencies in life, times of crisis, of doubtfulness, of sorrow. There are days when a man needs counsel, and days when he needs consolation. But with the recession of a faith such as Christianity bestows, the Comforter retires and the Counsellor departs away. So he must find that all those fountains of wisdom at which men have been wont to drink are dried, and that all the springs of relief are frozen at the source. In the Substance-Deity of Pantheism there is no personality, and therefore there can be no care, no compassion, no knowledge of our grief. To look to that shapeless and anomalous mass for any sympathy with suffering man, would be vainer than to talk to the electric fluid, or to invoke the vaporous drift of the open sea. Where tears fell fast as rain, they must continue to fall unregarded. Where sorrow bowed herself, scarce half-alive, upon the face or the relics of the loved and lost, there would she be suffered to stay, and there to harden to insensibility or sink in absolute despair. In time of doubt, no Counsellor; in time of trouble, no Comforter; nor any explanation of the riddles of life, nor any alleviation for its distresses. No sense of duty to constrain the rich; no trustful faith, no devout resignation, to mitigate the adverse lot of the poor. And so — to pass from private affairs to those of a wider range — the common, social life must remain in a state of confusion as thorough as that of the individual career, so far as any explanation of its course and intent and object are concerned. As for history, the man who has lost his creed and his faith must also give that up forever. Regarded as an intelligent solution of successive events, history would no longer exist. The world must be regarded as moving on without superintendence: no thought could be less reasonable, on this hypothesis, than that of an intelligent agent distinct from the world observing the drift of human affairs, and carrying on good and grand designs through the chances and changes of life. Thus, with the loss of the true faith, and upon the substitution for it of the weak philosophy and the vain traditions of men, there must ensue a gradual but sure disappearance of Almighty God. He withdraws from the life of the individual, from the life of the community, from the life of the nation, from the life of human kind. He ceases, He departs, and men are left alone. No thought, no care, no heart, no love, beyond ourselves. No law, no duty, no crime, no good, no evil. No aim in life, no joy, no hope for the future. No one to be grateful to, none to fear, none to offend. No blessing to ask, no curse to escape. No reward in toil, no fruit in labor; no hand to dry the tears, no ear to hear the prayer. No mission for nations, no honor for states, no object for citizens. No pious dedication of the infant, no creed to teach the child, no blessing of strength and grace for the youth. No divine sanction for the marriage relation, no obligations for hearth and home. No worship for the living, no sacraments, no intercession for the sick, and for the dead no psalm of life and immortality. No grace to say over the daily bread, no invocation ere we lay us down to sleep, no word of thanks for the dawn of another day. All gone. All that speaks of God, — all that implies God, — all that breathes of Him, or refers to Him, or derives its signification from Him, — all gone forever, like a dissolving dream. No Father, no personal Friend, no providential Guide, no Wonder-worker, no Inspirer and Hearer of prayer: all lost at once, with the loss of faith in a God distinct from the world, yet near to us; a spirit, yet personally like ourselves; Himself unchanging, and near to us all, as Creator, Redeemer, Sanctifier, — as the most august, the most complete of all existences, — even as the Father, the Son, and the Holy Ghost.

Alas! my brethren, where should we be left with all this gone? And what would that be worth to us which yet remained? Go it must, — all this to which we have held fast, all this in which we have trusted, — if philosophy should supplant faith. There is no faith, save one, — the faith in the Most High and undivided Trinity, "*One Lord, One Faith, One Baptism, One God and Father of all, who is above all, and through all, and in us all.*" To Him, as to our stronghold, let us turn, and let us cling with firmer grasp to our traditional belief in Him. God is no stranger here; and what we hold and profess concerning Him is no uncertain theory, no doubtful and hesitating experiment. We know Him well; we know Him as we know each other. It is He that hath made us, and not we ourselves; that hath made us of the dust, that hath fashioned us as the potter mouldeth the clay, so as that we are no part of Himself, albeit He is not far from every one of us, albeit He is through all, and in us all. But He who created us, and in whom we live and move and have our being, knows us, and observes, and has intimate and familiar acquaintance with everything about us, from first to last. There is no human knowledge to be compared with His in fulness; there is no discernment to be named in the same breath with His for precision. His thought embraces us and all our concerns, and His eye follows and investigates our every step. He, moreover, is our true home, — the One for whom we were made, — He whose glory is the end of our existence, and without whom the nations are as nothing, yea, less than nothing and vanity. All our strength is in Him, and from Him is all our hope. When He thought good so to do, He created us. And when we had fallen He redeemed us. And now that He has made us His own, He sanctifieth us. There is nothing upon earth so sure as the hallowed round of doctrine, truth, and usage, known as His revelation. It is all authentic; it cannot change or fail. While the statute books of nations have become antiquated and obsolete, the Holy Scriptures remain ever fresh and ever new. While the nations perish and cease, the Church still stands and renews her youth; for God is in the midst of her, therefore shall she not be removed. He is no vague dream, no impersonal substance. It was His Son, eternal like Himself, who dwelt here among us, and was called Jesus Christ; it was He who was nailed, in ancient time, upon a cross, and who died thereon; it was He that was buried, that rose again of a Sunday morning in the sweet spring-time, and afterwards ascended to heaven. In the Redeemer of men there was, of course, a personality as perfect and complete as there can be in men themselves; and that personality was the same which was from the beginning, is now, and ever shall be, the person of the eternal Son of God, eternal as to all the past, eternal as to the future. This is He whom we have believed. And while we recognize Him, hour by hour, in this mortal life, as, with the Father and the Holy Ghost, its Author, its Ruler, its Sustainer; so does this recognition ascend to a higher pitch of marvel and joy than any tongue could avail to express, when we contemplate the wonder of our redemption. For us He died; for us He gave Himself a sacrifice; and freely hath He thereupon given us all things to make that redemption available, to make that sacrifice our acceptable ransom. Ours is the whole system of grace, — a system adapted to all people and to every place and time, and bespeaking the Lord God in the most amiable and blessed of relationships, the Father, the Friend, the lover of His creatures. When we find comfort in the reception of the holy sacraments of the Church, it is because they are the links between Him and our souls. When, at the reading of His Holy Word, our hearts do burn within us, it is because His voice is speaking to our ears, because His spirit is communing with our spirits, because our eyes are fastened on the very syllables which His good hand hath penned. When, in the sanctity of the first day of the week, there comes refreshment to the weary spirits and bodies of those who then may rest, it is because that day is the everlasting prophecy to man of the Sabbath of God's eternity. When, seeking the calm shelter of the house of prayer, we forget, for a space, the din of the world, it is because we feel that He is there with whom it is good for man to be alone. The relief of confession of sin; the sweetness of acts of penitential discipline; the strength which slides down from above into the soul and spirit, in answer to humble, persevering prayer; the conscious joy in acts of mercy and love; all these, and the hundred more of such like emotions, are what they are, simply because God is what He is, and because we believe what He has told us of Himself, and because we know that He saith true. Ours, then, in so far as we are Christians, is the undying confidence in Him which alone can support us in all dangers, and carry us through all temptations, the realization of His presence, the experience of His power, the thrilling, sensitive response to the calls of His Holy Spirit, the trust in His strength, the veneration for His wisdom, the rejoicing acquiescence in His will. We make of Him an acquaintance, we picture Him to ourselves as a friend, we think of Him as of a neighbor; in Christ, He is become to us a wise, a good, a great, a glorious, a perfect man. There can be no vagueness in such a faith in God. There can be no wavering in principles such as these. There can be little doubt as to the future, — as little as there is of mistrust in the present. We know our calling. We can see ahead a long way. We look not to the future as a blank. It is an ocean, over which we have not yet spread our sail; but the Bible is our chart, and our faith is the compass, and we shall not fear as we launch forth.

Beloved brethren, the words which have now been said respecting that future towards which we are hastening, recall the necessity of finding a conclusion for these studies and, perhaps, rambling thoughts. How, then, shall the conclusion be made? By reflecting on the conclusion itself; on the conclusion of any earthly career, as it must appear upon the pantheistic hypothesis, or upon the analogy of the Christian religion. We have thought together of that dismal system which denies the personal God; which makes the universe eternal; which views God and the universe as substantially one; which regards all visible things, and man himself, as but evolvings of the primal substance, as but phenomena in a fated sequence of development. That system would be dismal when studied at every advantage, — by a man in full health, and rich, and free from care and responsibility, and at the hour of noontide, and amid scenes of outward prosperity and peace. Even then, the system would be almost oppressive in some yet uncomprehended awe and mystery of prophetic failure. How, then, must it appear, if all these circumstances should be reversed? How must these tenets sound, when spoken to the heart of poverty, of pain, of grief? How, finally, must this cup of consolation taste, when presented and offered to the lips of the dying? Go to the man whose hour is come that he should depart out of this world, and speak to him, in the name of this philosophy, such message as it can convey; and if there be a shadow darker than the shadow of death, these tender mercies of the pantheistic creed shall pour that hopeless shadow, broad and still, upon his forehead and upon his soul. There is no light beneath that shade; there can be no dawn beyond. Go to the man whose hour is come, and tell him that all is over forevermore; that he has played his part in the fatal sequence, and now must disappear eternally; that he was but a portion of the absolute substance, a manifestation for a moment, an evolution, and that the gulf which vomited forth the atom is about to engorge it again. Tell him that his whole course here on earth has been but a dream; that his consciousness was but the consciousness of a deep-heaving matter; that whether that portion which he calls himself shall ever appear again in realized form or conscious shape is utterly beyond the power of prediction; that life and time are but "an everlasting shore, that tumbles in the godless deep;" and that for him there now remains but this, —

> "To drop, head-foremost, in the jaws
> Of vacant darkness, and to cease;" —

tell him all this, the gospel of Pantheism, and then withdraw, lest the curse follow fast upon your footsteps from the lips of despair and death. Yet not, perhaps, the curse; perhaps the blessing, — yea, the blessing upon you, who, in thus exhibiting the last resources of Philosophy, in thus revealing in the most critical time her utter incompetency as a guide or a comfort, have been the means of awaking the soul from its delusion, and breaking the spells of Satan, though at the eleventh hour of life. Many a man who, through long and hardened years, has had no better hope than such as this, at the close of all hath yet, and, let us trust, not too late, recoiled from the awful emptiness in the face of which he had dwelt, and flung himself, in mortal extremity, in anguish of spirit, at the throne of the Father, and at the feet of the Great High Priest. Oh what peace and joy is there in believing! What perfect confidence in the will and power of the Christian's Saviour, of the Christian's God! And what calm triumph, in the final hour, over any and all fears of death! "*Preciosa in conspectu Domini mors sanctorum ejus:*" Precious in the sight of the Lord is the death of his saints. For them, the past life is a dear, a sweet reality: for there they walked with Him; there had they experience of His power; there they learned to love Him, and there they were made ready by grace for all that is to come. Dear are the friends they met; dear those whom they leave; nor is the parting over-sorrowful for nature to support, since presently they that are Christ's shall meet again. And if the past be real, (Oh very real and very sweet that past of a Christian life!) what shall be said of the future? No "vacant darkness" there, but the full and warm light of paradise. No awful emptiness, but the house of many mansions resounding eternally with the voice of joy. The Father's house,— the doors therein open, the pathway thither paved with pure gold, and the angels of Heaven descending and ascending thereon! The Lord, standing above, proclaiming to all salvation, and unto all peace. The children thronging thither to the feast of eternal days. This is the vision of holy death. All fear cast out in perfect love; all doubt dismissed in the filial confidence of the heart. Then the comfort of the Holy Communion, the body and blood of the Lord; the refreshment of prayer; the hopeful "farewell," being but for a little time; the commendation of the soul, made by the minister of the gospel of Christ. And then the stillness,—the stillness which is such on our side alone; which, on the other, is no stillness, but the blending together of the praises of the rejoicing hosts on high. And then the temporary sleep of the body in the care of our Lord, who is the Resurrection and the Life.*

O Father, Son, and Holy Ghost! high and undivided Trinity! To Thee, God in Three Persons, be ascribed all glory and praise! To Thee, O Father, do we owe all praise, for that Thou hast made us! To Thee, O Son, do we owe all praise, for that Thou, when we were dead, didst make us to live again! To Thee, O Holy Spirit, do we owe all praise, for that Thou dost convert us, and renew us day by day! In that great name standeth evermore the hope of the world; in that great name standeth our eternal life. And long after the prophecies have failed, and the tongues have ceased, and the knowledge hath vanished away, shall be proclaimed, yea, forever and forevermore,

"Lo! this is our God! We have waited for Him, and He will save us: this is the Lord; we have waited for Him, we will be glad and rejoice in His salvation."

* See Note H.

NOTES.

NOTE A.

Mr. Herbert Spencer's work on "Universal Progress," lately reprinted in this country, has appeared since these lectures were written. I could not have desired a fuller illustration than that which it affords of the tone and results of modern rationalistic thought. The term which best describes his system is "Mechanical Atheism." It is the negation of a divine mind and will, and the explanation of the origin and government or course of the world by matter and movement, by purely mechanical laws, and by the blind forces of nature. The pantheistic ideas of emanation and development appear in startling rigidity; the dogma of the creation is contemptuously flouted; Christianity is accounted for as a mere phase of feeling; and every vestige of religion, as we understand it, vanishes. Lest these expressions should seem too strong, I quote from a recent review of the work by a writer not known to me, in order that my opinion may be justified: —

"'Universal Progress' is the title selected by the author . . . . by universal progress he means a law of evolution common to all beings and all phenomena, whether material or spiritual. Many even of the so-called powers and forces of nature are developed by new combinations and conditions that have gone before . . . . the same doctrine is applied to what we call mental powers. These are only new and higher manifestations of what are usually called the vital forces, when brought into activity under favoring physical conditions; and these vital forces are but similar developments of chemical and mechanical powers, under their appropriate excitants, when interposed at the proper juncture."

No one can mistake the meaning of this who knows the history of the pantheistic philosophy. Let us hear the results of this " Universal Progress " theory in its applications to the grand and supreme questions of God, man, the soul, time, and eternity: —

"Of the object of religious worship Mr. Spencer says little more than we have hinted. In his 'First Principles,' he furnishes an elaborate argument, derived from his philosophy, to show that there is a one mysterious something, a somewhat, the object of worship, whose being is manifested in the universe, but whose nature and relations are utterly unknown and unknowable. His nature is unknown, because the nature of everything great or small is unknown, and is a mystery. His relations are unknowable, because that such a being should have relations is impossible from his very nature as absolute and unrelated. That there is such a being we know; but who or what he is we do not know, nor can we ever learn. Like time, space, force, and motion, he is; but what he is cannot be conceived by human thought. The apotheosis of his system is, to set apart and consecrate the universe as an altar 'to the unknown God,' whom all men must worship, but all alike 'ignorantly,' — whom, therefore, no man can conceive or " declare " to another. Before this altar each successive generation must prostrate itself in blind devotion, evolving for itself a form of creed and worship which the next generation must inevitably abandon and outgrow."

Such are the results of the latest theory of rationalism, — late in time, but in substance identical with the systems of the old pagan schools. I spoke of this scheme as " Atheism." But it is worse than Atheism in this, that, while it removes the true God from view, it does not leave the place empty, but puts in it a shadow and spectre of its own exorcising, —

a thing which means nothing, and serves no purpose except to deceive the minds of the ignorant. In the name of all that is fair and manly, we protest against this dissimulation; and we affirm that if these men were honest they would say at once what they really think, "There is no God." But they cannot say that, because such a declaration would kill their cause. Reason and revelation agree entirely in their estimate of the man who takes that position,—"*Dixit insipiens in corde suo, non est Deus,*"—and therefore our philosophers are wary, and feign this veneration for a "somewhat," to which they apply the sacred name, lest the people should call them fools.

NOTE B.

Historical Sketch of Pantheism.

FOR the satisfaction of those who would pursue the subject as careful students, I present a brief outline of the history of this great system.

It offers itself to us under two aspects, that of a religious dogma, and that of a speculative philosophy. The latter is a development of the former. As a dogma it appears in the religions of the ancient world; as a speculation it is dominant among the philosophies of later days. Under each aspect it has been the persistent adversary of revelation: in antiquity it filled, or tried to fill, the void left by the loss or defacement of the primitive tradition; while in modern times it has constantly opposed the religion of Christ.

Beginning with the earliest days, we find this heresy in India. The system of emanation, as opposed to the idea of creation, is the fundamental principle in the Indian theology. Brahma is not a creator, but all things emanated from him. The theological system of the Brahmins represents the universe as evolved from Brahma, and as reëntering into him again; he is the first and infinite substance, the cosmic

unity, and in the creation and destruction of successive worlds consist his life and death. (See the Vedas, and the Code of Manou.)

In the theology of Egypt we find the same idea of emanation, and we miss that of creation proper. (The student may refer to Herodotus, Diodorus Siculus, Plutarch, Iamblichus, and Porphyry.)

From the Indian and Egyptian systems, thus standing first, and exhibiting the pantheistic ideas in their more rigid form, we pass to those of Chaldæa and Persia, which exhibit modifications of the former principle.

In Chaldæa, dualism appears, a supreme deity being recognized, and, at the same time, an eternal, incorruptible, and uncreate matter.

In Persia the same dualistic idea presents itself, but the two principles are regarded as in antagonism: Ormuzd and Ahriman strive for the mastery amid ill-defined relationships.

We pass, in our survey, to the Greek religions. The subject is undoubtedly an obscure and mysterious one; and yet the old Orphic doctrines seem to be but a reproduction of the theory of emanation. But the older religious ideas, whatever they may have been, were lost in the materialism and humanitarianism which absorbed everything; and when St. Paul preached at Athens, it is evident that the idea of a God who created the world, and who governs it by His providential power, was lost to that generation.

The school of Thales was founded on the idea of a dualistic cosmogony, like that of the Phœnician and Chaldæan systems; while that of Pythagoras started with the theory of emanation, and, running through the common course of pantheistic principles, attained its full development in Timæus of Locris and Ocellus of Lucania.

The Pythagoreans set out with the idea that all existences are included in the Absolute Unity. Their teachings on the subject of the production of things are indistinct; or, if they teach at all, they seem to teach the system of emanation.

Xenophanes took up the question of the production of things, and, beginning with the denial of a creation *ex nihilo*, concluded that the universe is eternal, that there is but one substance, and that thought is the only immutable reality.

Parmenides adopted this principle, and pushed it into pure idealism, denying any reality to the finite, and saying that all things that we see are but an outward show, that there is no reality in phenomena, and that the testimony of the senses is but a delusion; he also maintained that thought and the object of thought are identical.

From this extravagant idealism a reaction occurred. Leucippus and Democritus founded the materialistic school.

Heraclitus endeavored in vain to find a means of harmonizing the idealistic and materialistic systems of the day.

Then followed the reign of universal skepticism.

It was when the mind had reached that wretched position that Socrates appeared, and reformed philosophy by confounding the sophists by his well-known mode of common-sense argument; by appealing to the love of truth and virtue which still remains, notwithstanding every disadvantage, in men; and by leading them back toward intellectual life. The movement given by him led to the rise of the great schools of Plato, Epicurus, Aristotle, and Zeno; and rigid Pantheism for a time disappeared from the scene.

But in the school of Alexandria the old heresy revived, and by the Gnostics and Neo-Platonists it was formalized once more.

The Gnostic philosophy had for its base the system of emanation. It had two branches, a unitarian and a dualistic. The unitarian Gnostics held one principle, from which all spiritual and material substances emanated; while the dualistic Gnostics affirmed two eternal principles, spirit and matter, of one or the other of which all beings are developments.

The Neo-Platonists aimed at opposing Christianity and staying its triumphant progress, by effecting a reconciliation of all the philosophies and of the religious traditions of the nations. It was an immense syncretism. They then proposed a theurgic system by which to place men in connection with the gods, and to reproduce, in a purified condition, the beliefs and practices of the old polytheism.

There were three chief centres of this sect, — Alexandria, Athens, and Rome. Its great exemplars and representative men are Plotinus and Proclus. These authors drew from the old Eastern sources ; the system of emanation forms the key to their whole philosophy ; and in their doctrines may be found the germs of the later and modern pantheistic theories. Giordano Bruno, Spinoza, the German transcendentalists, and the French eclectics, have but reproduced their ideas. Together with their blended system of syncretistic speculations there came a revival of polytheism, of the practice of magic, and of fancied communication with genii, gods, and departed spirits, just as, in the nineteenth century, while rationalistic principles have been gaining ground in the community, the practices and arts of the table-tippers, the rappers, the spiritualists, and the dealers with the dead, have become familiar to the public. It is impossible to miss the meaning of these correspondences.

Since the Neo-Platonistic school forms the connecting link between the ancient and the modern pantheists, it seems best to present the views of that school, in order that the genealogy may be clearly seen. Maret (to whose admirable and exhaustive work I am indebted for this historic sketch) thus sums up the philosophy of Proclus : — "There is only one substance in the universe, always identical with itself ; we discover this essence in ourselves by the contemplation of the *Ego*. This substance is the Absolute Unity ; it encloses in itself the principles of multiplicity and of diversity. The primitive unity, like a luminous mass, radiates from its eternal centre, and produces the infinite series of beings which are one and manifold at once. These derived unities are incessantly brought back to their centre by the same force which flung them forth like sparks from the fire of eternal life. Thus the world is perfect. Matter is an eternal emanation from God. Evil is a mere negation; it is but the inequality of souls."

Thus far of the Alexandrian school.

The triumph of Christianity brought with it a second decay and disappearance of Pantheism. It is not until the time of Charlemagne that we trace it again. In the ninth century Scotus Erigena revived it; and other writers of less note exhibit in their works the predictions of its future appearance. In the fifteenth and sixteenth centuries, however, the study of this philosophy was fully renewed, and schools were formed, the pedigree of which may be traced at once to the Neo-Platonists.

The appearance of Giordano Bruno and Spinoza upon the scene marks the commencement of the pantheistic revival. It is unnecessary to enter upon a full account of their tenets, which are already too well known. To reconcile those tenets with the Catholic faith would be impossible; their relation with the anterior philosophies is close and full; in principles and results they are the same.

Thus, descending the chronological scale, we arrive at the recent epoch when Germany became the theatre of the full development of the traditional heresy. Kant was the father of the modern intellectual movement in that country. Fichte, Schelling, and Hegel followed in his steps, completing his work. In Hegel Pantheism is once more presented, pure and simple, to the world. The line, from the Brahmins of India to these rationalistic philosophers, is visible, link after link. The metaphysical systems of Germany are but the old Pantheism clad in new forms. No essential progress has been made. At bottom we find the same tenet of the unity and identity of substance, the principle which was held by the Pythagoreans and Neo-Platonists, revived by Erigena, repeated by Giordano Bruno, and made the central point in the system of Spinoza.

As for ourselves, we are concerned, not so much with the

system considered in its scientific form, as with its applications. These are numerous; as, for instance, to morals, history, social order, art, religion. It is in these applications that we have to meet and deal with it; whether it present itself in the shape of the historic theory of Buckle, who strives to trace all events to physical causes, discarding the idea of a superintending providence; or in the form of the materialistic atheism of Spencer in his scheme of Universal Progress; or in the socialistic experiments of Fourier and his disciples; or in the rational religionism of those who dispense with creeds and sacraments and all the framework of a visible and historic Catholicism, pretending to serve God in individual seclusion without the mediation of rite or form or consecrated priesthood; or in the dreamy and unreal poetry and literature of the day; or in the feigned conferences, through mediums, with the spirits of another realm; or in the mad attempts at advance and progress towards the idolization of humanity. It seems impossible for any candid man to read the history of human thought without perceiving that one and the same disease runs through it, and that the course is ever in the same direction when the restraints provided by Almighty God are thrown away. There is and can be no new gospel; it would seem that there can be no new heresy. These, which now assail the truth, have risen up against it heretofore, and have been as often prostrated. In like manner the reaction will presently come, and they shall be cast away as abominable, and left to smoulder again in the ashes of their burning.

NOTE C.

I USE the word "licentious" in the sense of "unrestrained by law." It is strange that they who reprove lewdness in the flesh and in the carnal passions, seem to feel no need of restraining the mind from indulgence in speculation; for profligacy is one and the same thing, to the eye of God, whether it be that of the body amid harlots, or that of the intellect amid profane thinkers.

To the statement in the text that the mind gravitates naturally towards the pantheistic scheme, it may be objected that this is to represent the reason as tending, in its ordinary exercise, toward infidel solutions. But this objection is groundless. The reason, wrongly acting, must depart from the truth; but the reason, under the conditions necessary to its proper exercise, cannot go astray. For the reason is but an eye; and without revelation it is where the bodily eye is without light. It would be as great a misconception of our thought to say that the intellect, acting naturally, must incline to error, as to imagine us asserting that the natural use of the eye tends to blindness. The use of the eye under false conditions, as with insufficient light, or on very fine work, or in any way in which it was not intended to be used, would indeed tend toward the destruction of that organ. It is so with the reason, which, in divine and supernatural things, was not made to be used except under the illumination of the light of God. When men speculate by themselves, independently of that light, as shown to them in historic and outward revelation, they are misusing the godlike faculty, and do but weaken and ultimately destroy it.

NOTE D.

THE French school of Philosophy traces its origin to Descartes; the principles advanced by him were perfected by Malebranche, and it would not have been difficult, at that stage, to have harmonized the system with theology and religion.

But the sensual school of Locke took its rise in England. Its principles, adapted by Gassendi and Condillac, were thrown into the philosophical schools of France, which rapidly sunk towards materialism and naturalism.

Then came the Revolution, which upturned society, and shook the nation to its centre, drenching it in its own blood.

After that social convulsion the French philosophy revived, with a powerful reaction from the materialism of its previous stage,—a reaction which was due to the rise and influence of the German schools, idealistic and spiritual in their tendencies. The result was seen in the establishment of the modern eclectic school, of which Cousin was the founder.

The eclectic school denies the charge of Pantheism: it is, however, in its principles and results essentially pantheistic. A comparison of the philosophy of Hegel (about the character of which there is no doubt) and that of the eclectics, will show practical results of the same character. The historic systems, the moral systems, the psychological systems of France have grown up together with the eclectic philosophy, and as a result of the movement and impulse which it gave to human thought. The tendencies of those systems are all in the same direction; the breach between philosophy and religion is widening continually; and the minds of the educated men of France at this hour would seem to be in almost hopeless alienation from the faith. "The longer one lives in this country," says a writer now resident in Paris, "the more deeply does one become convinced of the hopeless divorce between intellect and faith. The lay mind is totally alienated from the Church and from revealed religion. There is more external respect for the former, perhaps, than for the latter, because '*les convenances*' exercise a very arbitrary power in France, and it is considered correct for women and children to be communicants. Educated men scarcely ever are so; even those who profess a kind of lax reverence for the Church and for religion tell you almost invariably that they do not '*pratiquer.*'" This is the recognized phrase, which seems to be regarded as a matter of course, an almost satisfactory equivalent for the service of God. When Madame George Sand paints a young man, a Parisian, son of a philosopher, who is a deist like his father, and at the same time pure and noble in his life and feelings, she gives us, I fear, an ideal picture, little in accordance with the facts; and, indeed, elsewhere in the same book she shows young Frenchmen as generally scoffing against humanity and moral principle. But she does not exaggerate the strength of the almost universal prejudice of the educated class against the Christian faith. I told you once before that one of the most Christian-hearted Frenchmen known to me, a literary man of note, told me not long ago that it was next to impossible for an educated Frenchman to be a Christian; that the utmost he could do was to 'aspire.'"

NOTE E.

THIS idea of a progressive, advancing, and improving God, blasphemously as it sounds to us, is among the most familiar of the pantheistic notions. It is expressed in the well-known formula of the Germans, "*Gott ist in werden,*" *Deus est in-fieri.* To show that the thought is not a strange one here at home, I make the following extracts from an article in a radical journal published in this city; the communication is a reply to the questions, "What, Where, and How is God?" The writer says: "God is the intelligent, vivifying principle, pervading and developing all matter. . . . . Eternal progress is one of the attributes of God, and is the coexistent fundamental law of the universe. All nature demonstrates this profound and all-pervading principle. God Himself cannot be exceptional to the universal law of which Himself is the enactive and vitalizing principle. Therefore God Himself progresses. God possesses sensation," &c., &c. This writer has but copied the ideas of the German pantheists.

NOTE F.

The Catholic dogma of the creation (using that word in its proper sense of bringing into being what was not in any way before) is, and must ever be, the test of all heresies touching the origin of the world. The philosophers repel the charge of Pantheism; they claim to believe in a God. But they will not admit that God is a creator. If, however, the dogma of the creation be denied, there remains no conceivable choice but between Dualism and Pantheism. Either God created the world, or He did not. If He did not create it, it is eternal. If eternal, it is either substantially distinct from Him, or substantially identical with Him. To take the former alternative is to admit two eternal substances; to take the latter is to hold the unity and identity of substance. There is no logical, no possible position for him who denies the Catholic dogma of the creation, save in Dualism, Pantheism, or skepticism.

NOTE G.

To the summary presented in the text it may be added that the system, as now operative, divides itself into two branches, materialistic Pantheism, and idealistic Pantheism. The former is a gross sensualism and naturalism, which sees in the universe nothing but matter and its modifications and transformations. The latter is a more elevated and more serious speculation. In the former, God is brought down to and absorbed in the world; in the latter, the world is lifted up and translated into God. But the grand and distinctive features in each are the same, — the denial of the distinction between the finite and the infinite, and the assertion of the unity and identity of substance.

NOTE H.

During the season of Lent, in 1863, when I was delivering these lectures, I received from time to time, through the mail, communications evidently written in great bitterness of spirit, denouncing my work in unmeasured terms, and especially reviling the dogma of the Holy Trinity. When the lectures were announced for repetition last winter, the attacks to which I have referred were renewed, and in divers communications, for the most part anonymous or bearing false signatures, I was assailed as an enemy of the truth, and the doctrine of the Blessed Trinity was aspersed, with a malignity which could hardly have been surpassed, while spiritual powers were appealed to and invoked as at hand to silence my utterances. I record these facts to show to what extent the simple enunciation of the truth may arouse the fury of the enemy; and also that I may notice a circumstance which profoundly impressed me at the time, which has been often referred to since its occurrence, and which, in view of the foregoing particulars, (known only to myself at the moment,) afforded, as I devoutly felt, a visible sign of the neighborhood and approval of the Almighty. At the instant of my uttering the words, "O Father, Son, and Holy Ghost," the whole congregation, as though moved by a more than human power, slowly arose, and so remained, with heads bowed in adoration, during the utterance of that which followed. Never did I feel God nearer than at that moment; and never did I feel more thrillingly the certainty of the ultimate triumph of the eternal truths of the Catholic Creed. It was as if a voice from heaven were crying aloud, "Unto me every knee shall bow, every tongue shall swear, saith the Lord."

THE END.

www.ingramcontent.com/pod-product-compliance
Lightning Source LLC
LaVergne TN
LVHW021421110826
845150LV00007B/2029

* 9 7 8 1 4 2 5 5 0 8 6 5 4 *